A BELLYFUL OF BLISS

FREEDOM FROM EMOTIONAL EATING
IS JUST THE BEGINNING

Amy Iverson Adams

CONTENTS

"Bellyful": (n), more than one needs, more than enough

"Bliss": (n), utter contentment, serene joy, euphoria

Introduction

Did you see the Oprah episode when actress Tracey Gold appeared with Rudine, a woman who was suffering with a severe eating disorder? In recovery from her own eating disorder, Tracey was encouraging Rudine to "make the little steps to fill your mind so that you can fight back...you have to feed your brain!" To which Rudine weakly pleaded, "But how? How do you do it?" I understand why Oprah said that Rudine's question is "one of the most powerful things she's ever heard." When Rudine asked "How," Oprah said it changed the way she approached every show from that moment on. This book is the "How".

How do you dissolve the desire to overeat? How do you pause in that moment of wanting to overeat and feel the comfort you are craving - without food? How do you stop obsessing over what you ate, what you shouldn't eat, what you really want to eat, the number on the scale, the size of your thighs? How do you become someone who rarely thinks about food? Is that even possible? How do you replace the constant head chatter with peace? How do you lose self hatred and gain a feeling of pride and respect for your body? How do you feel so full of comfort that the thought of overeating is absurd? In Part One, I'll tell you my story of how I discovered the six disciplines to freedom, and in Part Two, I'll explain exactly HOW you can apply the disciplines so that you can be free too.

I struggled, prayed, begged, read and asked "How" for fifteen years. I tried therapy, food plans, self help groups, psychiatric medication, rehab, Eye Movement Desensitization Reprocessing and hypnosis. I was willing to do anything to be free from the torture of my compulsive overeating. I watched girls become free from *their* compulsion, as I sunk deeper into a hopeless state of "what about me?" despair. I knew that if they could become free, so could I. I just didn't understand why, with all the effort, willingness and prayers, I was still bingeing, obsessed with food and, for years, overweight. I remember going out to eat with friends and being baffled at how they ate happily, and went on with their day. They didn't have to buy more food on their way home or obsess about what they just ate and how they were going to "undo it" by not eating the rest of the day, or by exercising or purging. They didn't hide at home feeling fat and afraid to be seen because no one would want them or love them being overweight. That's how I felt.

"Normal" eaters baffled me. Eating seemed to be just a small part of their life, not the majority and determining factor of where their life would lead, or stall. I also couldn't understand how overweight people could just decide to go on diets, lose weight and voila, done. I just didn't get it. My message to any of you who are losing hope: don't throw in the towel and say "I'm tired of the struggle, forget it, I'm just going to eat and purge or just be overweight". If you've been compulsively eating for at least a few years, becoming free does not happen overnight. But if you practice the six disciplines with even half the energy you spent eating, you will begin to eat less and love yourself more.

I'm no longer at the mercy of the binge. When I do eat more than my body needs, I don't fall into the cycle of obsession, deprivation and depression over what I ate or if I gained weight. I wore my favorite pre-pregnancy bikini and skinny jeans four months after giving birth to both of my children. I still can't believe that sometimes. No diets, trainers or gym memberships, and I eat the food I love. I have a light body and more importantly, a light heart. I never thought I could be naturally thin and healthy. I am and you can be too.

PART 1

BURYING MY BLISS

Chapter 1

When Freedom from Compulsive Eating was Free

"Blessed be childhood, which brings down something of heaven into the midst of our rough earthliness"   -Henri Frederic Amiel

I was a "normal" eater for fifteen years before the beast barged in. I consider my relationship with food "normal" because I really can't remember many thoughts or emotions attached to eating. I ate when I was hungry and I stopped before my stomach felt too full. I was naturally, effortlessly thin and healthy. I used food to satisfy stomach hunger just as you drink water to quench your thirst. I didn't look forward to when I could eat again or fantasize about what was for dinner. I rarely felt excited about eating and never felt guilt, shame or anger connected to food. Food and my feelings were separate entities, independent from each other. I had just as few thoughts and feelings about my body as I had about food. I can't remember a single thought or feeling about my body size or the way my clothes fit. Body image and food obsession simply did not exist in my brain. That's freedom.

The strongest memories I have about food are baking cookies and Rice Krispy treats with my mom. I loved pouring, mixing and cooking the goodies. To me, that was the fun – and licking the spoon of course. I also remember sitting down at the dinner table wishing it was over so I could go out and play. My mom usually cooked, and we always ate dinner as a family. My brother and I did the hiding-the-peas-under-the-napkin trick. I'd move the food around on my plate so it looked like I ate more than I did, because I was ready to get up and play. I associated eating with taking me away from what I would rather be doing. Sitting down to eat was like pushing the pause button on the fun.

When I was ten, I was in the buffet line with my cousin at a family reunion picnic. She was piling food on her plate and seemed really excited about eating. I watched her plow through two or three plates of food with zeal. I had never seen anyone get so excited about eating. After the cookout she ran up to an adult laughing and hyper and said "We pigged out!" I remember thinking, "What is she talking about? Why did she eat so much and why is she so excited about it?" I'd never seen such emotion attached to food. I also remember spending the night with a friend who sneaked a gallon of *Angel Food: Cookies and Cream* ice cream out of the

12

freezer and we hid in the closet to eat it. I was sitting in there with her feeling uncomfortable, thinking "Why are we eating ice cream out of the carton in the closet after bed time?" I was confused and homesick. I called my parents to come get me.

The other time I witnessed an abnormal encounter with food as a child was in my kitchen with my friend Vicki. She found the bag of chocolate chips in the pantry, opened it, and ate handfuls from the bag without asking my mom. It had never occurred to me to do that. I had no desire to eat plain chocolate chips. Yet. The only time I was even exposed to an excess of food, primarily junk food, was at my grandparents' house. They had a candy drawer and my brother and I would always raid it when we visited. We also loved to bake with my grandmother and lick the mixing bowl. Even then, I didn't obsess over or binge on the junk food. I just enjoyed a moderate amount. I was always a skinny kid, not "Olive Oyl" skinny, but thin, active and healthy. Playing and living in the moment was normal for me. What a sweet, free, precious fifteen years.

I was the average, well- mannered little Southern girl in a world where respect for authority was enforced and girls didn't get angry. I played, had fun with friends, but didn't have much of a voice. I often heard, "If you can't say something nice, don't say anything at all." I didn't come into the world owning my power or claiming my space. Many people with eating disorders are survivors of sexual abuse. I was never sexually or physically abused. No one in my family had an eating disorder. My parents went on the Weight Watchers diet once and lost a few extra pounds but never suffered with compulsive eating.

*****

You too were once a normal eater. Your natural, innate state of mind and body is freedom from compulsive eating. "Compulsive" is defined as: a strong, usually irresistible impulse to perform an act, especially one that is irrational or contrary to one's will. "Freedom" is defined as: the absence of necessity, a lack of effort, independence, liberation or deliverance from confinement or bondage. I invite you on a journey back to your natural state, your childlike spirit. You won't be fearfully exploring unchartered territory by eating only when hungry and stopping before you are too full. Maybe you began overeating as a young child. No matter how early your disordered eating began, you lived free from the mental obsession with and physical compulsion for food at an earlier time in your life. You can reconnect with your carefree, light, playful spirit of trust and innocence. Even if your trust was broken by an authority figure, you can learn to live from a new place of trust in the divine source of security and comfort that IS safe.

Most children aren't worried about financial security or the state of the nation. They're focused in the moment. Babies are good examples of emotional health. They cry when they feel sad or hurt and then it passes. They smile and laugh when amused and happy, then those feelings pass. You too can remember how to express your feelings as they come and let them go. Babies aren't self conscious. They have big bellies, chunky thighs and couldn't care less. I remember my mother- in- law offering my son a cookie while he was running around playing with his cars. He ignored the cookie because he was having so much fun playing. I was surprised because it was chocolate chip, his favorite kind. My children remind me that some days your body needs more food than others and that playing is always more fun than eating. There is a childlike spirit inside you just waiting to be awakened.

Your spirit is what animates your body. This supernatural energy is the vital force that inspires positive thoughts, feelings and actions. It creates the aura that exudes from your being. The energy that you unconsciously radiate is coming from your spirit. It's what you know and feel at your very core. I used to think of "spirit" as empty air or foggy smoke. What I've learned is that it's alive! It's movin and shakin! It's the vibrating creative energy where breathtaking sunsets and love songs come from. Your spirit inspires radical ideas to spring forth into the universe and revolutionize our human experience. I believe God puts a piece of its spirit inside every one of us at birth and it's up to us to stay connected to and nurture that piece of pure creative power and unconditional love.

Chapter 2

The Beast Barges In

"The most painful death is not the passing away of a body, but a body that remains alive while the inside dies."   -Unknown

At fifteen I began to be aware of my body. Being thin to look good became a priority for my friends and me. We compared our figures and secretly competed to see who could be the thinnest. I was about eight to ten pounds at the most from being "skinny skinny", so I began to have my first thoughts about dieting and exercising to lose weight and look better. I was five foot seven my sophomore year in high school when I made a New Year's resolution to "get down to 115 pounds and stay there". At this point losing weight wasn't an obsession. My mom took me to Weight Watchers and we decided to go to Jazzercise, per my request. I was excited about getting super skinny. That was the first of only two diets I tried. The next month after thinking about how "fat" I was, I decided to try a new diet where I planned on losing three pounds a week so I could reach my goal weight by the time summer started.

I turned sixteen that summer and any trace of my "normal eating" vanished. My Junior year of high school I started bingeing, restricting, not eating for a few days at a time, vomiting, trying to control what I ate, and became obsessed with losing weight though I only weighed 120 pounds. The normal eater I once was came and went as fast as a dozen donuts during a binge. Gone, lost, not to be seen again for fifteen years. Oh, I also started getting drunk every chance I could get and smoking cigarettes because, well, I needed relief. Smoking a cigarette after I ate made me feel thinner. My best friend, who was in the process of becoming anorexic, told me that smoking one cigarette burns thirty calories. It's obvious to me now that inhaling smoke into my lungs doesn't dissolve food in my stomach. Oh well. Back to the raging beast that moved in and set up shop inside me with no warning.

I know that my Dad's alcoholism and his and my mother's problems my Junior year created massive feelings of rage, insecurity and sadness that I was unable to express and were just too intense to feel. It's as if I automatically knew that eating a bag of cookies or a pint of ice cream would quell the storm inside. An instinctive coping mechanism maybe. My rage and hopelessness seemed too huge yet compacted to try to sort out and express, even if I had the opportunity. So I ate, and it actually helped ease the pain to a degree of manageability, until the feelings resulting from bingeing and purging became unmanageable. As I mentioned, I also used alcohol every chance I got because I loved the effect it produced in my mind and body. I desperately needed ease and comfort from the anger and turmoil. The feelings of fear and insecurity as a result of the problems my parents were having became unbearable. Alcohol and food were the only tools in my toolbox at the time. Getting drunk resulted in getting grounded for a month at a time. I spent most of my Junior year grounded and enraged at being trapped at home. The way I got through being trapped in my parent's house with intolerable feelings trapped inside me - was to eat, adding momentum to the destructive cycle. I felt such shame and fear of being seen bingeing that I would sneak as much food as fast as I could from the kitchen to my room. The ease I felt at the beginning of a binge was soon replaced with anger at myself and with the obsession over how I could lose the weight I just gained. My fear of being caught bingeing was realized at times when my family would catch me with the food, which just deepened the shame. I felt like they could see into the vulnerable place inside me that I was afraid for anyone to see. I was also afraid they would confront me and ask why I was eating so much, for which I had no answer. All I knew was that eating the food eased the pain for a moment. I could not open up and express that vulnerability. At times I felt better when I didn't vomit after a binge. Vomiting always felt like such a violent experience. Not just physically but mentally as well. It was as if I could feel all the feelings I swallowed during the binge being exorcised from my gut. But soon the feelings would awaken again and demand to be fed.

I managed to stay thin and miserably obsessed my entire Junior year and then my life took an unexpected turn just a few weeks into the summer before my Senior year. To celebrate freedom from a month of grounding, I started the night at a friend's house with a bottle of Peppermint Schnapps. I hadn't eaten anything in two days and finished the bottle in less that an hour. I was desperate for oblivion. I vaguely remember starting another drink and driving downtown to watch a Pink Floyd laser light show. I remember flashes of crossing into the opposite lane and hitting a few roadblock signs before fading to black.

I opened my eyes for a split second to see a strange man driving my car, then black.

My next memory is sitting in my driver's seat surrounded by a dozen shirtless, strange men staring at me. I tried to put a few words together, something to the effect of, "Where are my keys?" To which I heard laughter, name calling and "You're not goin' anywhere tonight." I'm grateful that I was so intoxicated that I felt no fear, just a slight desire to get away from what felt like a dangerous situation. After a few hours of taunting and refusal to let me go, I asked them to call my parents. They asked for my home phone number, which we'd had for ten years, but I couldn't remember it. They retrieved my driver's license and called my parents. My mom later told me that the phone rang at four am and when she answered, an unrecognizable man's voice said, "Do you know a girl named Amy?" My mother answered, "That's my daughter. " To which he responded, "Well, you better come and get her, I don't know if she's gunna make it." He gave my mom directions to the house, which was in a crime infested neighborhood in South Memphis. When my parents pulled up in front of the house, the men scattered, disappearing into the night. My Dad picked up my vomit covered body, laid me in the back seat of his car and drove me home.

I fell in and out of consciousness and came to the next day safely in my bed. The first moment or two I wasn't sure what happened the night before but prayed that the feelings of impending doom were from a bad dream. As I rolled over I felt hardened chunks of vomit in my hair and knew. Any trace of freedom was about to be taken from me.

I entered a thirty day adolescent drug and alcohol rehab a few days later and treated my painful feelings with the only available tool: food. I gained fifteen pounds in less than two months. I binged and purged with a vengeance. Back in high school, before "Dinner Dance," my school's term for "Prom," I ate only an apple a day for seven days because I was afraid to feel the shame of having a fat face in my pictures. I lost seven pounds. The day after Dinner Dance I ate with an aggressive sense of urgency. I had experienced the high of losing weight fast and the powerful feelings of control which I thought would motivate me to continue the restriction, but bingeing won out. I quickly gained more weight and more pain.

My freshman year at The University of Tennessee at Knoxville was a blur. I relapsed after a year of sobriety and made up for lost time within a few weeks. My drinking was more out of control than before because I had no restrictions. I was living away from my parents, which meant I could drink freely without their consequences. Relief at last! Soon I was drowning in the incomprehensible demoralization of my drunken behavior. Before dawn one morning I came to and noticed a stinging

21

sensation on the inside of my left knee. My skin was burnt and bubbling. I vaguely recalled riding away on a motorcycle in a toga from a fraternity party as my friends watched disapprovingly. I didn't recognize the guy passed out in the next room. I didn't know where I was and wanted to go back to my dorm. I felt afraid as I looked for a way out of his house in the dark. The floor creaked down the hall and I froze. I couldn't get the door unlocked when I heard a strange voice ask, "Where are you going?" Fear shot through my veins. I stumbled out the door into the front yard and called a friend. She found me and said nothing on the way home. I felt her judgment and my self loathing spread like a virus through my body.

I usually drank on an empty stomach and binged before passing out. I was bloated and embarrassed. For the next three years my weight fluctuated within a ten pound range. I was using alcohol and drugs, more than food, to treat my dis-ease.

Depression and hangovers kept me in bed and out of class. I failed out of college my freshman year and returned home to Memphis. I didn't believe I could excel academically despite having graduating from a fourteen- year exclusive private prep school. I worked dead end jobs that barely supported my pathetic lifestyle. I was fired from my minimum wage job as a receptionist for smelling like alcohol at work. It hurt that I was living below my potential. I didn't believe I had any gifts or talents to contribute to the world. I didn't see a future for myself. Getting drunk and overeating were my only means of feeling comfort, relief or a connection to anything. I was feeding the vicious cycle of hopelessness and depression. After swallowing a bottle of pills and slitting my wrists in a drunken stupor, I stood at the dead end of my twenty year old life. My life hurt. I was tired. I wanted to feel better. In a moment of grace, I considered what twenty-five would look like if I continued drinking and reluctantly decided to get sober.

*****

With a sober mind, I went back to school and studied Early Childhood Education. I worked as the Assistant Director of an after-school-care program and I made the Dean's List. During those four years my self esteem grew but I smothered my spirit with food. I was often obsessed and depressed and rarely felt at peace. I searched relentlessly for a solution to my eating disorder. My hope would rise as each new method offered freedom, and I fell deeper into despair after each binge. I was stuffing my body with massive amounts of food and further abusing it at times with vomiting and laxatives. I decided, after three years of working with children, that I didn't want to be a teacher.

I accepted a higher paying, dead end job doing clerical work at a Doctor's office a few months before I graduated from college. Feeling bored and trapped in an office building, the minutes seemed to pass like hours and oftentimes the only way to get through the day was to eat. Emotional eating usually turned into a binge and turned me into a self-centered, intolerant employee driven to numb my feelings with any food I could get my hands on.

I remember getting home one Friday night after work, having canceled dinner plans, knowing that I was in for the weekend to check

23

out. I was stuffed and sick from eating all day at work. It was yet another weekend wasted on sugar. I remember trying to hide in my bed from the demons swarming around me like vultures, reading Marianne Williamson's *A Return to Love*, hoping her words would stop the snakes from slithering around in my head.

I was willing to do anything to stop bingeing and obsessing over food. The anxiety I ate to relieve was sometimes like a low grade fever and other times it was a full on heart racing, palm sweating attack. I decided to try a strict food plan, abstaining from sugar, wheat and white flour. I did it for sixteen days, which were followed by a toxic binge on the seventeenth day. I tried weighing and measuring each meal but the rigidity of that program proved to be unsustainable for me. I tried defining my own abstinence, but I couldn't trust my insane head to make sane choices. I accepted the idea of being powerless over food. Clearly I couldn't stop bingeing despite my best efforts, but I was not convinced that I truly was, or forever would be, powerless over food. The concept of being "powerless over the first compulsive bite" spiraled me into destructive all or nothing thinking. A part of me believed that freedom lied in power over food. I was right, but it would take another few years to uncover that power.

*****

I began to wonder if it was trauma from my childhood that was subconsciously triggering my compulsion to eat. A friend had been successful at healing her eating disorder by releasing trauma with the help of EMDR (Eye Movement Desensitization Reprocessing). I was willing

24

to try it because I was so tired of my life revolving around food. My state of being had become unbearable and I saw no joy in living if my relationship with food didn't change. I had been struggling for nine years and begged God to let this be the end of my suffering. The EMDR therapist told me we could unlock the trauma stuck in my brain that was causing me to binge.

I sat on the sofa in her office and prayed for a miracle. I wanted to cry before we even started because I was afraid the EMDR wouldn't work. I went numb. Nothing was revealed. That was the beginning of the devastating despair that followed each unsuccessful method to stop bingeing.

One of my close friends had stopped bingeing through therapy and what she called "Gentle Eating." She was free AND thin. I was willing to try it. The therapist taught eating within the boundaries of hungry and full. She suggested using a hunger scale to determine when to eat and when to stop. She explained that a "1" on the hunger scale was starving, and a "10" was stuffed. The goal was to eat at a "2" or "3" and stop at a "6" or "7". This concept made sense to me. I was attracted to the simplicity of the direction to eat only when my stomach was hungry. I was able to wait for stomach hunger a few times but couldn't stop before I felt too full. My belief about love and deprivation was driving my need to "fill up before it's taken away again." I started to scratch the surface of why I felt compelled to eat and how to stop, and so began my bumpy road to freedom.

I began to see that temporary relief and the horrible feelings afterward sometimes seemed better than falling into a black hole, not knowing when I'd come out. At times I'd rather binge than feel alone and lost. I was so tired of food controlling my life and eating from my mind instead of my stomach. I wanted to live. I wanted food to be my friend, and fuel for my body. I wanted to trust myself and God. I wanted to believe that when I was overwhelmed with feelings of fear and discomfort, that everything really was ok, that I'm divinely protected and not alone. I needed to feel connected to people and God and feel like I was a part of the world. The thought of bingeing for another year or five or twenty was scarier than the feelings I was bingeing over. I wanted to be free to love myself and others. Bingeing had ruined so many beautiful days and had stolen so many opportunities. I began to believe I could stop with help from God and others. I once read that "Pain is the touchstone of all spiritual progress". I hoped that was true.

I gained twenty pounds following two leg surgeries. After x-rays, MRI's, and a needle biopsy on my left calf, the doctor diagnosed me with a cyst that he said could be removed by a simple outpatient surgery. During surgery, he realized it wasn't a cyst after all, it was a blood clot. What?! It also wasn't as "simple" as he led me to believe. Practically every complication that could have happened, happened. I actually ended up spending the next ten days in the hospital on a morphine drip and IV antibiotics. The doctor told me that the staph infection I contracted was because he left my leg open too long on the operating table and the surrounding tissue had died. Oops. Then my leg wouldn't heal properly. A team of infectious disease doctors, pulmonologists and surgeons couldn't

26

determine the cause of the problem. At one point, one of the doctors told my parents that if my fever didn't break within six hours, he would have to amputate my leg from the knee down because the staph infection was spreading into my thigh and they couldn't stop it. Nice. "Just a simple, outpatient procedure, you'll be walking the next day". I didn't walk for a month. Then I needed a second surgery due to further complications.

That nightmare began the week after I graduated from college. I always wondered what I would do for New Years Eve of 1999-2000. I never thought I would spend it in the hospital. Oh well, it's amateur night anyway, right? Before my surgeries, I was planning to interview for pharmaceutical sales rep positions because I knew a couple of people who were drug reps and I thought, from what they said, that I would enjoy the work and make more money than being a teacher. That plan was quickly derailed.

I couldn't exercise to burn off my binges and fell further into depression that being thin did not bring happiness or peace of mind, but being heavy hurt worse. After three months, I was off my crutches, out of my cast and walking normally. I remember before my surgeries, standing in front of my bathroom mirror, looking at my reflection in my size four black leather pants. I fit into my skinny pants, but I was such a prisoner that I couldn't even leave my house. In that moment, I knew that what I needed was much more than a thin body. It was obvious that food wasn't what I really wanted. I began to identify what might satisfy my spirit, which played an important role in how I later became free:

"I want to be free. I want to be independent. I want to find out who I am to the very core and wallow in it. I want to have a job that really feeds my spirit. Something in music. Heavy metal really opens up my soul. I want to experience exciting new things by myself so that they're all mine. I am under no one's control. I am the only person that is restricting myself. I don't have much money but I don't think I need much. I want to tap into my passion and energy and let it flow but I'm not sure how. I know that music lets my spirit soar. I don't want my fear to hold me back.

I want to take off, make a lot of money by myself and take care of myself. Bill (a producer friend at Ardent Records) suggested that I make a voice-over demo for commercials. I would love to earn extra money with voice-over work and really save. God show me my dreams today and how to make them a reality. I want to find a way to channel my passion and energy. I am no longer denying, ignoring or resisting my hungry soul. I want to feed it but I am not sure with what yet. I just know that there's a part of me that has been suppressed. I have not looked at this wild spirited part of me because I thought it was bad and not to be let loose. I want this part of me to live. I want to see what God is showing me about myself. I want to let myself be me! "

I began to experience a stronger connection with God and a higher tolerance for my feelings. It may seem obvious, but it took me a while to know that the feelings I ate over were always more bearable than the feelings after a binge. If I push them down with food they can't come up. My fear was that I would choke on the feelings. It's like vomiting. If

28

something is on its way up, it needs to come out. If I didn't let myself vomit when I needed to, I'd get sicker. I talked to a friend one night about fear and he said, "You get to a point where you are at the end of the light and you are looking at complete darkness. One of two things will happen: God will give you a solid foundation to walk on, or He'll give you the wings to fly".

Well, there's a lot of power in speaking your truth. A few months later, I did take off. I decided to leave Memphis, my home of twenty-five years, and let my free spirit loose! I embarked on my journey of experiencing exciting new things by myself and ultimately found out who I am to the core. You always hear that dreams come true in Hollywood. Mine did and they outshine anything on the silver screen.

Chapter 3

Tastes of Freedom

and

Dark Nights of the Soul

"Pain insists on being attended to, God whispers to us in our pleasures, speaks in our conscience, but shouts in our pain. It is his megaphone to rouse a deaf world."
                                                        - C.S. Lewis

After graduating from college and recovering from my leg surgeries, I accepted a friend's invitation to visit Los Angeles. I was hesitant when he first suggested a visit because he wanted more than a friendship and I didn't. When he described his suite two blocks from the beach, including the sofa I could sleep on, I finally agreed. I never thought about visiting Los Angeles but, what the heck? I was tired of sitting around my parents' house wondering what to do with my life. I had made my voice-over demo with Bill at Ardent Records, and packed a stack to take to LA with me.

Led Zeppelin's "Going to California" played on The Eagle, Rock 103 as I drove west across the Mississippi Bridge. I had read all of Melody Beattie's self - help books except for her newest release, "Finding Your Way Home". I listened to the Audio Version having no idea that I was doing just that. I arrived safely in Los Angeles a few days later. Sitting on the bluffs, looking out at the Pacific Ocean, I knew I was home.

Let's just say my first few years in LA were a bit rocky. It's a tough city to settle into, especially when you don't have a job and know no one. I landed in West Hollywood where the volume and intensity of my life turned up to a ten. I continued my desperate search for freedom from compulsive eating and most of it was a wild roller coaster ride.

I'll take you on my private tour of discovery and despair from Malibu to Hollywood. We'll spend a few nights at Chateau Marmont and many days hiking Runyon Canyon. We'll meet a super hero on my regular running route through Beverly Hills and we'll pray like my hair is on fire. My series of discoveries and revelations are what became the "How" that set me free. These disciplines were revealed through years of trial and error, exhilaration and terror. You'll witness my deepest surrenders and how I began to identify what I really wanted, if it wasn't food. You'll see that when I finally uncovered my beliefs (about everything) I found treasure in the possibility and power that I could change everything!

Getting sober five years earlier proved to be simple compared to becoming free from compulsive eating. The obsession with alcohol was removed, only to be replaced with a relentless obsession with food. Letting the lion out of the cage to eat a few times a day took years for me to tame. The mental slavery I suffered from kept me separated from the empowered life I suspected was possible for me. Spiritual practices that I discovered along the way provided comfort, hope and moments of freedom, but the tenacity of compulsive eating continued to thrust me back into depression.

The juiciest parts of my journey actually aren't the moments alone with certain rock stars and movie stars, but my moments alone with God. Yep, that's where it gets interesting. It's quite a story, how I got free, so I'll take you back to the Fall of 2000, my first, of many, falls in LA.

*****

My friend was staying at The Embassy, an old, beautifully charming hotel just two blocks from the beach and the 3rd Street Promenade in Santa Monica. I felt uncomfortable the moment I walked into his suite and saw the sofa just an arm's length from his bed. The "suite" he described was a tiny one room studio. I knew I needed to find another place to stay as soon as possible. I walked to a spiritual support group at 2nd and Wilshire Blvd. where I met some really friendly people. They asked me where I was staying so I told them about my discomfort with my sleeping arrangements in my friend's studio. When I said I needed to find another place to stay, Jay quickly offered his apartment, explaining that he was leaving in a few days to work in Alaska for a month. I couldn't help but laugh under my breath. I thought "Right! A complete stranger is offering me his apartment. He could be a serial killer." (Ironically, one of the FBI's most wanted fugitives, "Whitey" Bulger, was living directly across the street from The Embassy at the time. He would live there with his girlfriend twelve more years before a swat team surrounded the building and arrested him.) The girl standing next to Jay must have sensed my distrust because she added, "Oh, Jay's a good guy; he's just trying to help you out." To which I responded, "Well, thanks but I don't know you either. I appreciate your hospitality but can I sleep on it and get back to you? " He gave me his phone number and told me his apartment was in Westwood, a safe, centrally located neighborhood and I could come take a look the next day. Luckily, I had saved $4,000 from my part time jobs during my four years of college, so I could afford to pay him $500 for one month. I felt comfortable enough so I took a chance, gave him a check, and moved in the following day. I was relieved when I saw his boarding pass confirming his month long stay in Alaska.

I had a temporary home, next on the list was to find a job. My most recent work experience was doing clerical work at a Doctor's office and prior to that, as the Assistant Director of the after school care program. I didn't know exactly what I wanted to do, but I knew I wanted to work with adults instead of children and I would rather chew on glass than be stuck in a boring office all day. My prayer was for a fun job where I could help people improve their lives. Jay's apartment was on Malcolm Ave, just a block east of Westwood Blvd. I took a break from my job search one morning to go for a run, and as I ran up Westwood Blvd. a red lighted sign in a window caught my eye that flashed: "FUN JOBS". I went back after I showered and changed clothes and filled out an application for the Temp Agency.

Over the weekend, I met a guy who was friends with the owner of the famous "Rainbow Bar and Grill" on the Sunset Strip. He took me there the next night to apply for a job and when I walked in my heart skipped a beat. Signed photographs of my favorite bands covered the walls as the sound of Metallica blasted into my ears. I felt like I was walking into the party of which I'd always dreamed. Snapshots of Jim Morrison, Ozzy Osbourne, Guns N' Roses and Motley Crue surrounded me. The hope of actually meeting one of these guys was exhilarating. I could hardly contain myself! We sat down in a booth and the owner offered me a job waiting tables. I couldn't wait to start my first job in LA!

So, it turns out I wasn't a very good waitress. I was a bit forgetful, easily distracted and really just wanted to socialize. A table full of older men wanted to know where I was from when they couldn't understand my Southern accent. I told them I just moved from Memphis and was looking for an apartment to rent. When the man at the end of the table, who had just finished his fourth drink, told me I could move in on his lap, I knew that would be my last night as a waitress at the Rainbow. As a sober woman, working in a bar surrounded by raucous drunk men was just not fun for me. It was also difficult for me to stay up until three am. I loved going out for a good time but couldn't commit to working late at night in a bar four or five nights a week.

I didn't know what to do for work. I was envious of people who knew what they wanted to be when they grew up. Transitioning into adulthood

35

seemed easier for them. They went to college and slid into their career after graduation. Their financial security and sense of purpose was so attractive to me. Why didn't I know what to do with my life? I was a 25 year old woman with a B.S. in Early Childhood Education but felt claustrophobic when I thought about spending my career in a classroom. Having a degree to fall back on was comforting but the idea of being a teacher felt like I was smushing my round spirit into a square hole. I wanted to make enough money to support myself comfortably in Los Angeles. Was that too much to ask? Was that possible for me?

I needed a job. I also needed to find an apartment to rent. I had never rented a place before, except for a friend's guest house in Memphis, and I was overwhelmed. Parking tickets and binges were draining my savings. Eating to comfort my fear of not being able to support myself in LA drove me to seek refuge in a spiritual support group on Robertson Blvd in West Hollywood. It was a Saturday night and instead of exploring LA and enjoying new experiences, I had spent the past two days hiding in Jay's apartment in a fear fueled binge. As I walked into the group, I saw Joanie, a beautiful blonde speaking with clarity and confidence about self love and empowerment. It was just what I needed to hear. I was full of self loathing and felt defeated by the insatiable beast within. I couldn't hold it together and for the first time I cried in front of a group of strangers. Joanie introduced herself and invited me to go have coffee. I told her I'd love to talk but I didn't want to keep crying in public, so she suggested we go to her apartment right off Melrose on Curson Ave. I was embarrassed for being an emotional wreck. As I followed her white Acura Integra, it occurred to me that I'd never met a stranger in the midst of a breakdown.

I didn't make friends easily and this felt too intimate. She met me during one of my most vulnerable moments and she was offering support. I was accepting it. I needed a friend.

When I walked into her living room and saw the crown molding, hardwood floors, and arched doorways, I said to myself, "I want to live in an apartment like this." I loved the charming 1930's architecture with the colorful Spanish tile in the kitchen and bathroom, and the pull - open floor to ceiling windows. She told me that her live in boyfriend was on a golf trip in Palm Springs with his friend Eddie Cibrian. She and John had been dating a couple of years and they had both just graduated from law school. I explained that I just graduated with a teaching degree, didn't want to teach, and drove to Los Angeles on a whim. I told her I was looking for a place to live and a job although I didn't know what I wanted to do yet. Joanie seemed to have it all together: a nice apartment in a cool neighborhood, a boyfriend and a promising career practicing law. We talked for a couple of hours and on my way back to Jay's in Westwood, I felt comfort in knowing I had just made my first friend in Los Angeles.

Joanie called a few days later to check on me. She had talked to her boyfriend and they decided to offer me their second bedroom if I hadn't found a place yet. I couldn't believe it! I loved her apartment and only hoped to live in a place like hers one day. I gratefully accepted the offer. Joanie and John had been having problems for a few months and two weeks after I moved in, they broke up and he moved out. 434 North Curson would be my home for over two years.

In 2000, the Melrose-Fairfax district was an eclectic mix of nice Orthodox Jewish families and pierced, tattoo covered twenty-somethings aspiring to be the next big actor or musician. There was also a sprinkling of people like my roommate, who were just beginning a stable career and people like me who were still trying to figure it out. It was a colorful neighborhood and I felt right at home.

*****

It was a hot Sunday morning in September the first time Kent flashed his eyes at me. I had walked across Beverly Blvd. to the La Brea Tar Pits and spotted him kneeling down in jeans and a white wife-beater. I noticed him as soon as I walked in the room. He was the kind of guy I was instantly attracted to: tall, tattoos, and dark hair, exuding a slightly dangerous sensuality. I needed to know him. His energy drew me closer, becoming so intense that I quickly walked away. As soon as I got home I overate to settle the sexual energy he stirred up in me, and to numb the regret of walking away. Feeling grounded again, I walked out my front door and almost ran right into him! There he was walking his dog in front of my apartment. Kent lived right behind me on Sierra Bonita Ave. I had just met the man who would become my best friend, to this day, fourteen years later.

Kent and I shared a lot more than just fiery chemistry. We were both spiritual seekers who were willing to try anything to quiet the noise in our heads. We studied Eckhart Tolle's *The Power of Now*, listened to Deepak Chopra lectures and sweated it out at Earth's Power Yoga at the corner of Melrose and Fairfax. Our connection was deep and our acceptance of each other's madness was broad. As much as I loved Kent, my eating disorder came between us. We had plans one morning to go to breakfast for his birthday and I flaked. I had binged the night before and was too depressed to even answer the door when he came to pick me up. Too ashamed to tell the truth, I lied and said I slept through my alarm and the doorbell when he called later that day. Years later, he became one of two men I opened up to and shared the pain of my eating disorder. His unconditional love reminded me that I wasn't alone even when I felt like I was floating in outer space.

UNCOVERING, DISCOVERING, DISCARDING

Could 20 Pounds Make or Break My Life?

Being overweight in LA highlighted the dramatic contrast of how different I thought my life could be if only I was thin. I once again sought comfort and guidance from a food support group. A member asked me what it meant to me for me to be fat and why I wanted so badly to be thin. I told her that in my mind, fat means that I'm ugly, sloppy, and lazy. It means feeling not part of anything social and fun. It means no dates, no freedom, unattractive clothes, depression, and no swimming. I told her it meant not liking my body, dreading getting dressed and hating shopping. I knew women who were heavier than I was who were beautiful, sexy and successful. They had confidence in their body that I never had even when I was thin. My problem wasn't being over weight, it was how I abused my body with bingeing and the corrosive self hatred that followed.

I also told her that in my mind, being thin meant looking good. Looking good meant feeling good about myself and knowing that men were attracted to me. Thin meant freedom to go anywhere with anyone wearing anything I wanted and feeling pretty and sexy. Thin meant career opportunity, loving myself, my body and being proud of the way I look. Thin=freedom.

That's how I felt and what I thought at the time. I was still under the delusion at times that if only I was thin, I would feel great and my life would be great. I had forgotten the moment of truth the year before, looking in my bathroom mirror feeling miserable and trapped in my size four black leather pants. A heavy heart in a light body hurts. Pain bled into my body from my head full of fear. I looked good but I was a bloody mess inside. I wanted to look good, feel good, and be at peace. I wondered if that was even possible for me.

PUTTING THE HAMMER DOWN

I was so full of fear because my thoughts were scary! I hated myself every time I binged but I began to put down my hammer of self hate and try a little self love. Forgiveness became the first discipline in HOW I became free. It felt a lot better and I didn't need to punish myself as much with food. I began to see myself as the scared little girl I was and I started to take care of her. It's unsettling when you realize that you don't trust yourself. I decided, as Eckhart Tolle suggests in *The Power of Now* to separate the "me" who hated "myself". I could trust the loving spirit that observed the fear driven ego demanding to be fed. When I actively focused on my powerful nurturing spirit, I became a little more attached to it than to my fear based ego. My spirit grew as my fear shrunk, just as light dispels darkness. When I woke up in the morning, instead of hating myself and saying "Oh God, it's morning", I started saying things to myself like:

"Good morning, you ate everything yesterday and then more. You smoked. You're twenty pounds overweight and I love you anyway. You did those things because you were scared. You're safe. Take the next loving action just for today. I love you even though you binged and feel ugly and fat. You are beautiful."

One of the loving actions I took was treating myself to yoga classes. My introduction to the LA yoga scene was a level 2/3 class at Maha Yoga in Brentwood. The beautiful, light- filled, airy studio is the yoga home to the most perfectly sculpted bodies in LA. Despite the glowing, friendly faces, I felt a bit intimidated in my average, chunky body. To say that I was unprepared is an understatement. But when I saw the twinkle shine out of Steve Ross' eyes, I relaxed and felt like a welcomed visitor. Steve is the founder of Maha Yoga and was my first yoga teacher in LA. When he cranked up the music and the heat, his blissed-out, hi- energy exploded into the room and touched my soul. I'm sure he has that effect on most of his students, which is why his classes are always packed! Despite feeling like my body was not good enough compared to the "perfect" bodies, the intense workout followed by peaceful meditation kept me going back for more. Maha Yoga was a place where I could access my inner power, if only for a few moments, in the midst of burying it. Steve's class was, and remains, my favorite in LA.

41

*****

The "Fun Jobs" Temp Agency sent me for an interview at Celebrity Service on the Sunset Strip, right across from the Viper Room. Celebrity Service was an agency that provided celebrity contact information to Entertainment Industry insiders. Our clients were by membership only. For example, a booking agent from the Tonight Show would call us to get the contact names and phone numbers for Johnny Depp's agent, manager, or Publicity Rep. I was an "Account Executive", which just meant I answered the phone and looked up celebrity contact information from our database. I quickly realized there was nothing exciting or glamorous about looking at names and phone numbers on a computer screen. There were a few clients from magazines and TV shows who I became friendly with and enjoyed talking to. I did have a thrilling Hollywood moment one afternoon when my boss asked me to call our contacts to update our database. I picked out the celebrities that I liked and when I called the phone number beside Charlton Heston's name, a deep, faintly familiar voice said, "Hello?" I responded with my usual script,

"Oh hi, this is Amy from Celebrity Service. I'm calling to update our contact information for Charlton Heston".

"Yea, this is he."

"Oh,.. CHARLTON?!"

"Yes, can I help you?"

OH, UUUUMM, Hey! So this is the right number for you, I guess"

"Yes".

"Oh... Ok, Thanks so much, have a great day!"

"Yea, you too"

"Ok, Bye."

I still smile when I think about my phone call with Charlton Heston.

The dazzle of working on the coolest, most happening strip of Sunset Blvd soon faded when the reality settled in that I once again felt trapped in a dead end job that barely paid my bills. I hated being an underachiever. I remember lying on the floor during my lunch break in an empty room next door bingeing on chocolate, wondering what my purpose was and why I felt so lost.

Gazing out the window across Sunset Blvd. one morning, I noticed what looked like a party on the roof of the Bel Age Hotel (now The London Hotel). I was daydreaming about having fun and socializing in the sunshine with them when I asked my coworker what was going on up there. It was still early and I didn't think anyone was having a party yet, unless they were still up from the night before. She said they were filming a movie and all the people standing around were "Extras". I asked her what "Extras" were and she told me they were the non-speaking actors who filled in the background of film sets. I'd only been in LA a few months and hadn't seen a movie set yet. She told me anyone can do "Extra" work and it pays pretty well. My eyes popped open, I looked around my office and asked myself why I was sitting "here" when I could be "up there". I had no desire to become an actress but after a few months of sitting in an office, I was ready to try something new. The idea of working in different locations with a variety of creative people appealed to me. After a quick visit to Central Casting, I was booked on the Matchbox 20 video: "Mad Season". Witnessing the making of videos, movies, commercials and TV shows was fascinating at first. On the set of the hit TV show "ER" one day, I couldn't believe the hospital was on the Warner Brothers Lot. As far as the entertainment industry was concerned, I was a clueless 25 year old Southern girl waking up in the middle of Hollywood.

Believe it or not, waiting seven hours to sit for 30 minutes of filming inside an airplane on the set of "View from the Top" starring Gwyneth Paltrow, was about as exciting to me as watching grass grow. The reality of Extra work was sitting around on the floor for hours, waiting for your "fifteen minutes" that usually got cut on the editing room floor. The problem for me with sitting around all day was the ever present Craft Services. Craft Services was the free, unlimited feast of junk food that I couldn't resist. I ate so much on the set of a Britney Spears video that I hid in the dressing room to avoid being in front of the camera. I was supposed to be in a dancing scene at a club but was disgusted at the thought of seeing my stuffed body next to pretty, skinny girls. It was just another day I felt I wasted by eating and hiding, and it was my last day as an "Extra".

I updated my resume and signed up with the Temp Agency again. The only interviews they set up for me were for receptionist or assistant positions. I guess all I qualified for according to them, based on my college degree and work experience, was basic clerical work. So I went for an interview as an assistant to Larry Flynt. Oh yeah. I never thought I would work for "Hustler", but there I was in his office building on Wilshire

Blvd. I needed to pay my bills. I felt uncomfortable walking down the dimly lit hallway. It felt eerie, like an empty funeral home. No one was in the hallway, every door was shut and it was silent. So I walked into Larry Flynt's suite and sat in his private waiting room. After about ten minutes of thinking, "Why am I here? I have no business even working in an office in the "adult" industry", I looked around, grabbed my purse and made my escape. I ran down the hall to the elevator, feeling like I was in the middle of a B movie, and breathed a sigh of relief walking out the door into the sunshine. I quickly stopped in the middle of the crosswalk to avoid being hit by the Rolls Royce driving into the parking lot. There was Larry Flynt in the backseat. I guess he was coming back to his office for our interview. I thought, "I just stood up Larry Flynt." Oh well. Being associated with him just didn't seem aligned with my life purpose.

*****

It seemed like whenever I opened my mouth, people would laugh and say things like, "Why don't you do voice –overs? You're sitting on a gold mine". Clients I talked to at Celebrity Service, various assistant directors and actors on set when I worked as an "Extra", and a few celebrities I ran into encouraged me to do voice- overs. I ordered a yogurt at a yogurt shop in the valley one day and the guy behind me smiled and said, "Is that your real voice? You should do voice-overs." It was Corey Feldman. I met Andy Dick in West Hollywood one night and he raved about my voice and insisted that I could get a lot of voice-over work. So the question was, how do I get started? I was told to get an agent. Sounds easy enough. Oh, ok. Lemme just run out and get one. That began my frustration with my

45

"voice-over career". I spent a thousand dollars of my savings and made a more professional demo. A friend introduced me to Maurice LaMarche, a successful voice-over artist who was represented by an agent at International Creative Management (ICM) in Beverly Hills. He set up a meeting for me with his agent. I couldn't believe it! Was this my lucky break? Actors kill to get a meeting with an agent, and at ICM, one of the best in the world?! I sat in the waiting room, demo in hand and noticed another demo sitting on the coffee table. I picked it up. "Nicole Kidman: Voice-Over". Like I had a chance. Well, I didn't. In order to get an agent, you need to be a working actor, and to be a working actor, you need to have an agent. Over the next few years, my neighbor Estelle Harris, who played George Costanza's mother on "Seinfeld", and Slash, the legendary guitar player, said I had the perfect voice for voice-overs. They both encouraged me to pursue working in the industry. So the frustration continued every time someone told me how much money I could make doing voice-over work, without being able to get a foot in the door.

*****

As I mentioned, Los Angeles can be a tough city to settle into, especially if you move here knowing no one. It's not easy to make friends and plant roots in a big spread out city where people are constantly moving in and out. Something must have been looking out for me because I happened to fall into a pretty special crowd.

A friend invited me to Josie's Thursday night hangouts at his apartment on Olympic and Crescent Heights. Ten or fifteen of us would sit around his living room in candlelight smoking cigarettes, drinking coffee and connecting. Sage was always burning. I walked in late one night and as I scanned the room for a seat, a new set of piercing blue eyes met mine. Our spirits connected and I knew him before we met. I remembered him from nowhere but we knew each other. Pierre was one in a million. Larger than life. He was a tall, dark haired, handsome French Canadian who filled every room he entered. He was so much fun. Everyone wanted to be around Pierre. He spoke four languages, drove racecars, flew helicopters, played guitar and had a heart of gold. He made me laugh to the point of tears. One night we stopped to get gas on our way out to dinner and when he went inside to pay, he ran straight into the glass door-on purpose. He loved taking friends for sushi to Matsuhisa on La Cienega. Once, during dinner there for a reason I can't remember, he stood up and dropped his pants in the middle of the packed restaurant to reveal ridiculous bright aqua blue underwear. Being friends with the owner kept us from getting kicked out. He was crazy fun. The only time in my life that I've woken myself up laughing was dreaming about him. We were cracking up trying to define a word that I wish I could remember now. What a gift that laughter was when many mornings I woke up and cried.

Pierre was one of the few men who recognized the brain under my blonde hair. He said he heard wisdom in my voice deeper that an ear could hear. He "got" me. He and Kent were the only two men to whom I could confide the shame of my eating disorder and feel complete acceptance. Pierre understood from personal experience. The love I felt from him was a precious, rare, platonic love. He supported all of my efforts to become free from bingeing, including an inpatient stay at an eating disorder rehab in Texas. He gave me a bear hug and wished me the best as I left the Coffee House on Sunset. I made no progress in Texas. I didn't binge because the food was locked away but the mental obsession and compulsion to eat never subsided. I experienced no breakthroughs and returned to LA disappointed but relieved to be home. I was excited to see my friends and called Pierre. When I hung up the phone, I had a feeling that he was in trouble. He didn't sound like himself.

I went to work that day at DDK, a kid's talent agency in Burbank, right next door to Warner Brothers. I was working as a receptionist with the possibility of becoming an agent-assistant. I had no interest in being an agent, but again, I didn't know what my career purpose was and I needed to pay my bills.

For some reason, I decided to go home for lunch. It was a quick fifteen minute drive down the 101 at that time of day with no traffic. I walked into my apartment, thought about Pierre, turned around and walked right back out. I intuitively knew to drive up the hill to his house and check on him. I passed Yamashiro and suddenly felt nauseous. As I approached the top of the hill, it felt like a force was pushing me back. My car slowed. Anxiety trembled in my chest. Something dark and heavy was happening. I turned the corner and saw the white coroner van parked in front of Pierre's house. His front door was open. I walked up the stairs and saw him. He was lying in his bed. He had overdosed for the last time. As the coroner zipped him up in the body bag, it occurred to me how strange it was to see a dead body move.

Pierre was a diamond sparkling in the rough of my life. He was also an addict. He was a brilliant mind who was too smart for his own good. I miss him.

I lost hope after my unsuccessful stay in rehab and fell into a deeper depression after I lost Pierre. Glaciers of fear kept me blocked and separated from love. I was afraid that if I let myself feel my feelings, I would cry and people would see me being open and vulnerable. The loss of control was terrifying. Not knowing when the tears and sadness would stop kept me frozen. I felt so small compared to my feelings that I was afraid they would swallow me up and take control over me. At this time, I couldn't open up to people, but I could open up to God:

"God, I am so fu##ing angry and afraid. I'm angry that I can't stop eating. I'm angry that I eat instead of being with you. I'm angry that I still try to fix my feelings with food. I'm angry that I look fat and people don't like me as much when I'm fat. I'm angry that you let me have this food problem. Why can't I just be a normal eater and naturally thin? Why does my sobriety have to be so painful and difficult? I feel close to hopeless. I am scared that I'll keep bingeing and keep feeling not good enough and not taken care of. God, I'm pissed. Please fu##ing give me the power to stop. I'm afraid that if I don't fix myself you won't – you'll forget about me and let me suffer. God, I'm afraid to stay in this place of medicating myself. My spirit is sick and broken. My wings are broken. I want to fly. I want to depend on you. I want my connection to you to be my #1 priority. Are you even there? If I totally look to you will I be alone? Will I wither away and die? Will I be taken care of? Can I be free? Will I ever be free?

Are you listening? Do you care? Fu#k! Am I even supposed to be writing to you? How can I make it through a whole day and night without overeating or smoking? I'm afraid to be raw, real and vulnerable. I'm afraid I'll stay raw and vulnerable. God help me. I want to feel peace. I don't believe that I can get through a day without eating or smoking. Maybe it's the fear that you are not enough – so I need food and cigarettes. God, please take me to a place where I believe you are taking care of me and you are all I need. Please make my relationship with you more important than a quick fix from food and cigarettes. I want to smoke now and quit tomorrow. Damnit! Please make me God seeking instead of self seeking. I believe I've struggled enough. Please give me the willingness to let go of my old ideas. Please direct my thoughts. I keep trying to not eat and not smoke so I'll be skinny and loved and it's not working. I feel crazy. Please help me to see the truth. I do not have the power to repair my wings. Please fix my wings so I can fly and be an angel. I want to be rid of self. God, please reveal the truth about whom and what you are to me. I've written so many times and not been freed – Why? Is it because my motives have been to look good so I'll get love and approval from others? – Yes. I have gotten love and approval others before and it hasn't made me whole and complete or at peace. God – I know that only you, not a pill, or booze, or a man, or food, or cigarettes, or a city or a best friend, or money can make me feel whole or give me peace. Delusions have dominated my life. If I smoke right now would it negate everything I've just said? Do I know the truth from the false? Is my ego screaming? What's in me besides my ego? Will I be an empty vessel if my ego is gone? What would that feel like? I can't kill my ego but God, it's killing me. My ego breaks my wings and that hurts. Broken wings. I'm stuck on the ground. I'm not free to fly. My world is small and limited. My vision is narrow. God, can I go with you? I can't stop myself. I have the best of intentions but I don't have the ability or power to live up to them. That has hurt me. You do have the power. How do I get it? To stop playing God. OK. To stop using things to fix me. Ok. I don't have to power to pause and ask you – do I? Is this it? I have paused for a few minutes. God this feels like torture. I am mentally tormented. My spirit is crying and I can't make it stop. It hurts my ears. Please make it stop. My spirit is broken. My wings are broken. How does it feel to fly? Is it scary? If I do fly, will I break my wings again and crash? I feel paralyzed. God – I've wanted to be different for eight years. Is tonight any different? Am I full of shit? Please fix me. When my spirit cries – I need to quiet it fast. But I just make my spirit unconscious – that's how it quits crying. Food and cigarettes knock it unconscious for a while so it can't cry out – for a while. Then it wakes up and starts crying again. Sometimes I let it cry and you don't quiet it fast enough – so I have to. I can't stand for it to cry. It's too loud. Can I let it cry? Maybe it needs to. My spirit is sick. My wings are broken. My spirit must be healed before I can fly. I keep killing it slowly. How long will it take for me to kill it? I can't make myself stop. My mind races so fast that I react without thinking it through. I don't have the power to stop my head. Do I? Is my sick spirit fueling my mental engine? If my spirit was well, would my mind be insane? God, take me from this world. My spirit is everywhere I go. Knowledge of my spiritual sickness won't keep me from trying to fix it – but I'm killing it. I'm fu##ed. God, will you heal my spirit? Can you make me whole? Can you keep me from

51

smoking and eating so my spirit will have a chance to be healed? How long does it take to heal a spirit and mend wings? Do I have wings? I think I had them when I was a little girl – maybe I didn't. Have I ever been free? I remember not ever even thinking of overeating, smoking, drinking, using. Was my spirit healthy back then? Babies' spirits are healthy, I believe. Will I wake up in the am crazy? Can you heal my spirit overnight? I don't need to fly right away – I just don't want to cry. Please make my spirit quit crying. Will I be able to remember all this? Is this the truth? Am I full of shit? I want to be quiet and peaceful. I want to be conscious of your Presence all day and all night. Please take all that's in me that's covering my spirit. It's suffocating. Please take all the junk – all the ego driven fear and resentments and let my spirit breathe. God, please breathe life into my spirit. It's probably smothering. Is your will for me to suffer more so that I'll surrender? I don't know. What is your will? Maybe I don't need to know. Maybe I could intuitively know and have the power to do it. God. I'm flailing about. Am I ok?"

*****

UNTANGLING THE KNOTS IN MY HEAD

I began to uncover a whole system of negative and limited beliefs that were at the root of the fear infesting my life. Identifying my beliefs became one of the disciplines in HOW I became free from compulsive eating. I asked God to enable me to see the truth about my current beliefs that cause pain in my life. I wrote about sleep, food, hunger, my body and my emotions. I also wrote a list of what feelings I was avoiding when I ate. Identifying my beliefs and putting them on paper enabled me see in black and white why I was full of so much fear. A friend told me he did this same writing exercise and replaced old beliefs with new ones and chunks of his fear dissolved. I believed him. I knew that was **possible** for me. He gave me a few prayers that I prayed daily to help me through the process:

"God, please take me to a place where I am gladly ready (willing) to give up these things (food and cigarettes) for a better relationship with you."

"God, please help me find in you what I'm looking for in food and cigarettes."

So far, I had uncovered the truth that what I really needed was greater than food and I had uncovered the fact that fear was causing me to binge. I knew that the only thing bigger than my fear was God.

*****

When I was in fourth grade, I spent the night with my best friend Laney. I loved her family because they were so fun and crazy. One night her Dad was being silly and said I needed a lobotomy. I thought it was a funny word so it stuck in my mind. I would remember how right he was years later. My actions with food were crazy but the insanity in my mind was the engine. My friend Kent suggested that I could be restored to sanity but it would help if I would describe "sanity". It always helps when I have a target to shoot for. Once again I asked God to direct my thinking. After much consideration, I decided that if I was sane, I would have a clear mind that thinks straight. I would have the power of choice in my attitudes and actions. I would choose gratitude and faith. My actions would make sense. I would effortlessly do the next right indicated thing. I would be complete. I would be in touch with the unshakeable peace within. I would be in touch with my intuition. I would know what to do and do it. Sanity was simplicity. Clear headed reason. I believed God could restore me to sanity so I made this vision of sanity an affirmative daily prayer for a few months. It started to work.

*****

As desperate as I was for sanity in my mind and in my relationship with food, my craving for wild and crazy men remained. Joanie and I were driving through our neighborhood one day when we spotted four or five hot guys on motorcycles. Joanie was not shy. She yelled and hollered at these guys as I slinked in my seat. I wished I could exude confidence, especially around men, like she did. They yelled back at us, we got out of our car, and I guess her confidence rubbed off on me because I hopped on the back of a complete stranger's motorcycle. He popped a wheelie and we sped away. I don't know what came over me. I'm a smart girl but I just couldn't help myself. He screeched to a stop at each stop sign and popped a wheelie at every start. It was exhilarating! They invited us over for a party that night but we were both busy and never saw them again.

Motorcycles, especially Harleys, had a way of pulling my free spirit out of my prison of a body. Driving east on Melrose one day, I stopped next to a beautiful Harley at a stop light. When the driver looked at me his face appeared just as beautiful as his bike. "Nice bike." I said. "Wanna go for a ride?" he asked. "Yeah" We pulled over and I gave James my number. I was surprised when he called. My taste in men was very specific so even though attractive men were a dime a dozen in LA, only a few piqued my interest. I rarely felt comfortable enough in my body to open up to men because I was usually stuffing it with food. Staying shut down protected me from being hurt, which I believed was inevitable. I didn't date much and often felt overlooked by men. I took a risk and went for a ride with James. I remember the peaceful feeling of surrender as we winded down Sunset Blvd. to Pacific Coast Highway listening to Radiohead's "Creep". When we got back to his house he pointed out his brother, Hillel Slovak in original photographs of the Red Hot Chili Peppers. He was the first guitarist in the band and died from a drug overdose.

I also saw, for the first time, what looked like gun shot marks along the side of his black Lincoln Navigator. He saw me looking concerned, laughed and showed me that they were just sticker decals. James made me laugh. He was flirty in a playful way and I was attracted to the darkness lurking just below the surface. We had fun that day and when he dropped me off at home, he invited me to go on the "Love Ride", the annual fundraiser sponsored by Harley Davidson, to be led by Henry Fonda. I casually agreed, trying to conceal my burst of excitement. I couldn't wait to spend a day or two on the back of a bike with a guy I really liked. Anxiety and sadness crept in when the weekend drew closer and he hadn't confirmed our date for the "Love Ride". I was feeling the familiar pain of disappointment in what felt like abandonment. I sat across from Joanie smoking my cigarette feeling weak and rejected. When I told her he hadn't called, she was appalled. "What do you mean he hasn't called? The "Love Ride" is tomorrow, right? What a jerk!" I was taken aback by her gutsy reaction. I always felt like a powerless victim when men flaked but her reaction woke up truth in me. I thought, "Yeah, that jerk!" It was as if I expected to be treated poorly and was usually surprised when men did what they said they were going to do. I had high hopes and low expectations. She told me I had to call him and confront him. I learned growing up that girls weren't supposed to call boys and that idea lingered into my twenties. I also avoided confrontation like the plague, especially with men. The thought of calling him to ask why he invited me and never followed up stirred up an intriguing sense of power inside me. Who was this part of me who was considering standing up for herself, to a man? Joanie stood next to me, hand on her hip, foot tapping, until I finally picked up the phone. My hands were sweating as I dialed his number. My voice weak, feeling like a little girl, I asked him if we were still going on the ride in the morning and he sounded stoned when he said he'd forgotten about it and had to work through the weekend. Joanie was mouthing the words "Why didn't you call, bastard?", so I casually stated to him that he should have called to cancel. He took me out to dinner the next week to "make it up to me" and that was the last time we went out. I'll never forget my surprise at Joanie's insistence that I confront him and stand up for myself. I learned so much from her about straight forward, direct communication.

We were best friends. We were also roommates. No matter how much you love your roommate, issues inevitably arise if you live together long enough. I remember Joanie telling me straight up that I didn't contribute enough to our living space. She was buying most of our shared items and I needed to step it up and contribute more.   That was all there was to it. She wasn't really angry at me and there was nothing passive aggressive about her communication. One of her needs as my roommate wasn't getting met and she simply asked for what she needed. I respected her ability to unapologetically speak her mind. I also admired her independence. I wanted those qualities she had inside. Her powerful drive to succeed professionally was also an example for me. I didn't want to be a lawyer but I did want to be committed and determined to excel in a career that I felt passionately served a purpose.

When Joanie bought her first house, I rented my first apartment on my own. I couldn't afford much, so I moved into a tiny studio on Orchid Avenue right behind the Kodak Theater. Every time I walked into the front door of the old Hollywood Building I thought of Toby from "The Shining" riding his tricycle down the long hallway. On pink walls hung paintings of 1930's movie stars who watched me as I would come and go. The sound of helicopters hovering over Hollywood and Highland regularly forced me out of my apartment into the safety of my car. I spent many nights driving around in despair over the state of my mind and body. I smoked, prayed and listened to a lot of Alice in Chains. Listening to "Dirt" helped me feel not so alone when I was "Down in a Hole". I felt like Alice in Chains and other great bands understood my suffering, and their music was a salve on my wounded soul. Driving down Sunset Boulevard, I watched skinny girls dressed up having fun with guys, and I felt separated by food and fat. I was a 26 year old pretty girl who was watching life pass me by through the windows of my Honda Accord. As I wondered how much more misery I could stand, I drove up to Mulholland and thought of the tortured souls who couldn't take it anymore and turned their steering wheel just a little too hard and flew off the cliff. I knew I wasn't going to do that but my last resort of going into an eating disorder rehab failed so I was feeling hopeless. I remember saying to God as I looked out at the LA city lights, "I don't see how I can take this much longer. If this is some sort of trick, it's a dirty one, or some sort of experiment to see how much suffering one can stand then I get it, and I can't take it anymore!" After I purged my morbid thoughts of despair, I heard a whisper as I drove down Laurel Canyon that came from my mouth. I literally heard my voice whisper, "I still believe." And you know what? I'm convinced that miniscule belief kept me moving forward on my path to freedom during my darkest days.

After this particularly dark night of the soul, I considered moving back home to Memphis. My job at DDK ended when my boss closed the agency and moved to Florida. I didn't have the strength to try to get another dead - end low paying job, which was all that seemed possible for me at the time. I was mentally exhausted and emotionally drained. My bank account was also drained. Most days felt like such a struggle. Trying to get through a day after Pierre died without bingeing, purging or smoking was almost impossible. My demons had defeated me. I felt lost and alone living in the middle of Hollywood with no apparent purpose. I needed to collapse at my parents' house before I could get it together again.

I spent ten months in Memphis soaking in the comfort of home, family and community. I was so grateful to have the opportunity to regain strength at my parents' house. I got a job with "Screenvision" selling advertising space on movie screens to local businesses that showed in theaters before the movie began. I was still bingeing, but less than my last few months in LA. I felt more connected to friends and family, but I sensed that my potential for possibility in a career was in LA. I had no hard evidence to back up this idea; it was just a really strong feeling. As each month passed, my vision of a future in Memphis shrunk and I again longed for the possibilities of a larger, more diverse life in Los Angeles.

My spiritual progress in Memphis was again, two steps forward, one step back. With each step back, I reached out for God. Each step back was an invitation to experience God more. And each time I asked God for more, he delivered:

July 2003

"God, I need to feel your presence. I am full of fear and it feels like no one can help me. I've never been in a place where it feels like I don't have someone to talk to for direction. I know I need you. I want to believe you are enough. I need to feel your power. I want a clear channel of communication with you about what steps to take at all times, in all things. Please change my beliefs. I want to depend on you and not live in fear. Please open me up and direct me to what you would have me be. Please blow away the limitations I've put on you. Please dissolve my agnosticism about being taken care of financially. I want to be of service and be paid knowing I am doing what you have for me to do. Please make me conscious of your presence."

*****

I missed my friends, my spiritual community, and the pulsing creative energy of the big city. I missed the beach and the mountains, the 70 degree sunny weather. I realized that I felt more at home in Los Angeles, where I had lived only two years, than in Memphis, where I had lived 25 years. I prayed for God to give me clarity. Moving back seemed financially irresponsible. Staying in Memphis felt like I was containing my spirit. I was afraid of making the wrong move. I asked God over and over during this time of indecision to "remove my fear and direct my attention to what he would have me be". When I read that prayer from a spiritual book I found it interesting that it stated,"....have me *'be'* "instead of "do". I didn't know what that "be" meant. It seemed that knowing what God would have me "be" was less effective than knowing what God would have me "do". So I asked God to show me what it means to have him remove my fear and direct my attention to what he would have me *be.* I had a strong feeling that my life was waiting for me in California. I planned my trip back and set a date of departure. I got a tune up and oil change for my car to prepare for a safe trip cross country, again. I remember sitting in the middle of my bed one night telling God that I wanted to do whatever his plan was for me. I wanted to be of maximum service in my life and whether that was in Memphis or LA, just make it clear. I asked for a neon sign that I couldn't miss.

The sound of the wind rattling the windows woke me up. I looked at the clock. 5:15am. The sound of pouring rain lulled me back to sleep.

CRASH!!!!!! I popped out of bed to the sound of shattering glass. As I put my slippers on I smelled green. I walked down the stairs to find a tree lying across the entry hall. I looked out the front door and saw my car buried under a fallen oak tree. I guess I wasn't driving back to LA anytime soon. I was in the midst of the Superstorm of 2003 that left 70% of Shelby County without power for weeks. Winds over 100 mph left Memphis a disaster area. I had my answer. I wasn't under the delusion that God hit Memphis with a storm just to give me a message. That's ridiculous, but nonetheless, I had my answer. I surrendered my plans and went about my life.

I met Michael at a party at my friend Laney's house at Horseshoe Lake. There was something really sexy about him that I couldn't put my finger on. Maybe it was the Jim Morrison- with –short- hair look he had going on. I noticed him watching me as I stood on the table singing to Billy Idol's "Rebel Yell". Wait, he was really hot and he was really looking at *me*. I was always surprised when a guy I was attracted to showed interest in me. We had an intense three week relationship. I took a risk and opened myself up to him because I knew he couldn't abandon me since I was the one leaving, as soon as my car was fixed. My heart hurt for him. His Mom recently died and he was drinking daily. The night before I drove back to LA, I went to his house to say goodbye. The "goodbye" ended up being more of a conversation about why I didn't drink, how I got sober, and how I can look like I'm having more uninhibited fun than all the drinkers. I told him my story, the good the bad and the ugly. Our conversation ended with him telling me that he was really grateful to have met me. He said that I inspired him to be a better person and that he was considering getting sober. He also said that he'd never met anyone like me. He said it wasn't anything I had said or done, it was just the way I *was* that touched him. As I drove away I felt gratitude, knowing that the month getting my car repaired from the storm wasn't wasted, I had been a positive influence in Michael's life. Then it hit me like a ton of bricks: "God, please remove my fear and direct my attention to what you would have me *be*." Michael had just said, "It wasn't anything you said or did, it was who you are." What?! I knew God had just answered my prayer. Fireworks went off in my head and I felt shivers throughout my body.

*****

I made the trip back to LA and spent the first couple of months with Joanie in her new house in the San Fernando Valley. I can't even remember what I did for work those first few months, probably just sporadic temp work here and there. I loved living with Joanie but I was spending way too much time and money on gas driving from the Valley to the life I knew in West Hollywood. I reconnected with my friend Jackie one night at a party at her condo in West Hollywood. She mentioned that her roommate was moving out and told me that she couldn't see anyone else but me living with her. I was flattered and relieved, almost to tears. I always loved Jackie and had a lot of respect for her. Her condo was off Doheny Drive and just south of the Roxy on Sunset. It had a view of the city, floor to ceiling windows, a terrace, two bedrooms and a loft. Oh, and a washer/dryer, pool, sauna and parking. She offered her second bedroom to me at a price that I could afford. It was too good to be true, but I moved in and lived there for two and a half years. She was a fiery red-head who confidently spoke her mind. Her dead pan sense of humor made me belly laugh on a regular basis. I don't know why she never did stand- up. She was very opinionated and could put a spin on a story like no one else could. Jackie was also dramatically expressive. Her own

62

almost life size paintings of sparkly, voluptuous women covered the walls of the condo. I admired her ability to use her left brain to practice law and use her right brain to create dazzling art. I wondered if I would ever find my professional purpose and manifest my creativity as successfully as she did. I found it interesting that both of my roommates in LA were strong women who practiced law and practiced standing up for themselves in their personal lives. They were fantastic examples of independent women who I had the privilege of knowing on a daily basis.

After I settled in at Jackie's my eating disorder grabbed me by the neck and shook me like a rag doll. Relentless bingeing followed and I continued to purged the pain on paper. At least I had a great place to live.

*****

During this time an acquaintance offered me a job as a sales rep for handbags and accessories in the fashion district. "Fragments" was one of many showrooms in Downtown LA. I was grateful for the job because I needed to pay my bills but I had no drive to sell anything that I did not feel passionately about. I didn't care one way or the other if someone bought a handbag. I respected the creative process of the designers but lacked the motivation to sell. I had no interest in the fashion business and knew it was just another temporary job that was not in alignment with my life's purpose. I didn't know exactly what I was supposed to be doing, but as the months passed, I was absolutely positive that it wasn't fashion sales. I felt depressed and off track. Sneaking food at my desk was humiliating but eating felt like the only way to get through the day. I was overweight and the discomfort I felt about my body was amplified because I was surrounded by hip, skinny women who always looked stylish. If I didn't feel bad enough about my body already, the much awaited sample sales that the other girls took advantage of made me feel less than and more out of place. Whoever determined that sizes two and four were reasonable "samples" should be fired and replaced with someone who has a healthy body and a sane mind.

Anyway, I dreamed one night that my manager called me into her office and said, "Let's talk. You don't seem to be enjoying your job lately. I'm not sure if you are a good fit here. What do you think?" I knew I was about to be fired. I felt anxiety in my chest and the fear of being fired for telling the truth was matched by the fear of lying to try and keep a job I hated. It was a moment of truth. It was as if God told me in my dream to tell the truth and have faith that there is a better job for me, that I won't go broke and become homeless! As I was holding the tears back, I admitted that she was right. I didn't feel like I was a good fit for the fashion industry. I immediately felt a sense of relief. When I woke up I had a feeling my dream would be realized. I prepared myself to have faith and tell the truth.

About ten days later my manager called me over to a desk in the corner of the showroom. She said, "Let's talk". I couldn't believe it. Wait...was this really about to happen? She said I didn't seem very happy at work and asked me if there was anything I could do to increase my sales for the month. I was afraid that if I opened my mouth to answer I would cry, so I said nothing. She said I didn't have the "image" or the "interest in trends" that was necessary for the job. My moment of truth in my dream flashed before me and although I was afraid of the financial insecurity that would accompany losing my job, I knew that I could have faith and tell the truth. I felt like God's was sitting next to me holding my hand, and at that moment I made a choice to tell the truth. I admitted to her that I didn't think I was a good fit for the job either and felt the same relief as I felt in my dream. She then gently asked, "What kind of job do you think you would like to do?" The disarming kindness in her voice dissolved the barrier between manager and employee. I swallowed the lump in my throat and said that I wasn't sure but something along the lines of helping people - in a personal way. She didn't fire me that day but by the end of the week I gave her my two week notice. I walked away knowing I was no longer aimlessly floating in career space.

*****

A wise person once told me that the best way for me to forget about my problems was to help someone else with theirs. Since I was now jobless, I had plenty of time to be of service. A friend who was newly sober came over to talk to me about some issues she was facing. After I shared my experience, strength and hope, we chit chatted about other things. When I told her I was looking for a job along the lines of counseling or social work, she suggested that I call her friend Jeff. He was a therapist who worked at a drug and alcohol rehab called Renaissance, in Malibu. I called Jeff and went for an interview to be a Resident Assistant. As I approached Zuma Beach, I imagined commuting almost two hours a day from West Hollywood to Malibu and back and knew that 20 miles down Sunset and 20 miles along Pacific Coast Highway would be a pleasure. Driving, listening to music, and, I'll admit, smoking my cigarettes was one of my favorite pastimes. As far as commutes were concerned, this would be the best, hands down. It sure beat the drive downtown and back every day.

Statues of two white lions guarded either side of the gate at the entrance to the estate on Morningview Drive. I was buzzed in and drove up the hill, passing the horse stables and pool house, and parked in front of the oversized infinity pool. I got out of my car and was blown away by the ocean view. This place was over the top. Immaculately manicured gardens surrounded the property and a tennis court in the back provided a convenient outdoor sporting alternative to the indoor gym. Geez, what a place to get sober. And not a bad place to work either! I accepted the job at twelve dollars an hour with a chance for a raise after three months.

Paying for gas ate up a lot of my paycheck but I didn't mind living frugally, now that I felt my job served a significant purpose in my life and others' lives. My job description upon hiring as a Resident Assistant included answering the phone at the front desk in the majestic entry way overlooking Zuma Beach (on the marble floor, between two swooping stair cases). The extra wide front double doors were usually left open, allowing a salty ocean breeze to flow through the house. House? No, this place was a 14,000 square feet mansion. The gold touches throughout, the flamboyant statues and the iron fences tipped the scale from grand to grandiose. A bit gaudy for my taste, but I loved working there. My job description also included making sure the clients made it to their scheduled activities throughout the day. I helped with miscellaneous

66

chores like cleaning up after meals and taking clients to meetings outside of the house. I can honestly say that I enjoyed everything about my job. I didn't mind cleaning up after the clients. I sometimes pretended like it was my house and I quickly felt right at home in Malibu making twelve dollars an hour! The comfortable, laid back vibe of a small town beach community that I felt was very different from Malibu's reputation as being an elite, snobby, closed circle of the privileged few.

Right before the Ventura County line sat the second Renaissance property. It was an ocean front three story beach house, also with a pool and hot tub. It was a much smaller (well, that's easy) Spanish style house. I was really grateful when my manager acknowledged the good work I was doing and gave me more responsibility and a raise. I had the honor of leading meditation groups and various recovery groups, as well as taking the clients to the monthly sweat lodge at the top of Mulholland Drive.

Well, wherever I went I took my compulsive eating with me. It felt like dragging a twenty pound "Hefty" sack of manure behind me. The fully stocked gourmet kitchen provided free meals, which was a perk, but I couldn't resist the temptation to binge in a weak moment when no one was looking. As I've mentioned, in practicing spiritual principles like forgiveness and surrender, I did experience respites from the tenacious grip of compulsive eating. But because my spirit was buried under years of toxic beliefs, my progress was two steps forward, one leap back. I was slowly muddling through my messy mind in a nonlinear way to become free and clear.

A NEW DECADE OF POSSIBILITIES

July 2004

"I'm considering the **possibility** of actually making it through the morning without overeating. I'm really tired and zoned. I ran into Olivier in Beverly Hills Friday night and he spoke to me first. I was so relieved because he was one of the people who showed up to the June 4th party I invited him to, rang the buzzer, and I didn't answer because I was in the fat and depressed hole. I felt so guilty and ashamed. I lied and said I had the flu. Can you believe I planned a party at my house, invited people, then couldn't even answer the door because I was so depressed from bingeing? That's outta hand. God, please open my mind to how easily possible it is for me to be abstinent as a lifestyle. I want to believe that I deserve it. I deserve love. I deserve a man who loves me immensely. I deserve a thin body that I'm proud of. I deserve to feed my body healthy food. I deserve to look great in my clothes. I deserve happiness. I deserve peace of mind. I'm sitting in the conference room of Renaissance and it is breathtakingly gorgeous. The ocean is calm, as I would like to be. A red speedboat just drove past. I want to be on that boat wearing a white bikini and red shoes with a man I am in love with. I deserve fun – and the freedom to be me to my potential."

Sayonara twenties, Hello thirties!!

I spent the night before my 30th Birthday working at the beach house. When I first arrived in LA, at 25, I overheard a girl say, "I love that I get to work in Malibu. I pull over and watch the dolphins, because I can!" I thought to myself, "She's so lucky. I want to be able to do that!" As I reflected on the positive aspects of my twenties, I was grateful that they were spent sober, in LA and on a spiritual path of healing. As I looked forward to 40, I hoped to be able to say my thirties were free from bingeing and smoking. Better yet, I hoped to be able to say I was happy. I created a mantra for my 30th year as I listened to the waves crash below me: "I want to be happy – I deserve to be happy – I deserve to be at peace". As I closed my eyes to say goodnight to my twenties, I thought, "I love that I get to work in Malibu. I pull over and watch the dolphins, because I can."

I woke up at the beach house on July 19th 2004 a 30 year old woman. As I lay on the sand at Point Dume to start my thirties, I thought: "I can do whatever I want today. I love my life. This is the best day ever. I am happy. I am at peace. Someday my husband and I will take our kids to the beach – I'll hold one and he'll hold one and we'll walk out into the ocean."

TASTES OF FREEDOM

At this point, I had spent a few years uncovering, discovering and discarding. What I was about to find out was that I had only scratched the surface. What I would find buried deep inside was excruciating, gut wrenching pain and a blissful, exhilarating peace that I had never known before. Two therapists, a famously notorious bad boy, and a superhero named Goldie took my hand and led the way.

As I delved deeper, I began to experience highs at a level before I had only experienced pain. The highs were as intense as the lows. How I could continue to binge, knowing the pain it caused, baffled me. I knew that the first bite of a binge cut off my connection to magic, love and life. I could feel my channel to God's power becoming blocked. I was always left in shameful isolation. On the other hand, the light inside the freedom I was experiencing was so bright that I had to look back to the dark. My eyes took a while to adjust to the light. In my inability to balance the energy, my therapist Mina asked me what happens when I feel great and what I can do to stay grounded. I told her:

"I feel bliss, freedom and so much energy inside me that it sometimes feels like it will sweep me away. I feel intense desires to express myself sensually. I feel wide open to outside stimuli – especially men's attention. When I feel really good about my body it shows and I do get male attention. I have become over stimulated and felt carried away and out of control. I have binged to come down and block the channel to all the good energy. I want to feel love intensely and stay grounded and in control of the flow instead of becoming overwhelmed. Praying for centeredness and balance, drawing boundaries with men and letting loose with the appropriate man at the right time would work better. Praying for mutual respect balanced with attraction would help. Breathing deeply will help me stay grounded."

Turning 30 felt like being shot out of a cannon. I was lighter and flying freer than before. I was opening myself up to male attention and enjoying this new sense of power. I continued to seek freedom and continued to ask God to heal unresolved pain. I never imagined Matt Dillon would be the catalyst to heal my Daddy issues but there he was, standing inside my hula hoop on Melrose Avenue asking me for my number. The next couple of months were INTENSE! I'll just tell you the whole story-well, most of it.

August 2004

"I just got home from Chateau Marmot – with Matt. I am pleasantly surprised. He made me laugh but I don't think he meant to – which is really nice – very attractive. I'm sitting here wondering if he's really famous. He's so normal and I wasn't even nervous. Hanging out with someone after the first time I meet them can have moments of discomfort – weird silence – etc. That didn't happen. I'm a little surprised that I felt so comfortable and natural. Interesting. His tough New York accent and his deep voice really turns me on. There's something in his eyes that's intriguing. I'd like to know more. I think we'll go out again – that seems like the natural next thing. I'm also so pleasantly surprised at how cool he was when I didn't jump in the sack with him. He was pretty respectful. How nice! We listened to old jazz records and drank root beer. I'd really like to see him again. I actually really kind of like him. I have to get up at 6:30 in the am – that's gunna be tough."

September 2004

"I ran all the way up Runyon from Hollywood Blvd at sunset. When I got to the top it was dark except for a red haze on the horizon at the ocean – absolutely awe inspiring. I was the only one at the top and I lay down on the dirt on my back and tears ran down my face. I felt universal energy from the earth. I love my life."

71

*****

"Matt called last night – we went to sushi on Ventura Blvd and hung out at Chateau Marmont. It was really fun. When we got back to his suite after dinner he threw me up against the wall and frisked me – it was so hot I almost collapsed. (I had just watched *Crash*) I can hardly believe how comfortable I feel with him and how much I really like being with him. I'm fascinated. Whatever it is behind his eyes is drawing me in. I really want to stay open and not think about how much pain I'll feel when I don't see him again. I'm taking a risk here – Oh well. I'm gunna have fun while it lasts. Maybe it'll last longer than I think."

*****

"I woke up this morning to Matt's voice on my phone. His message made me shudder. Dear God. I love that he's direct and communicates. It's nice to hear that he's had a good time and wants to see me again."

I had amazing sessions with my therapist, Darcy, while I was seeing Matt. She was lifesaver. I got clarity about relating my experience with Matt to my Dad. The reason it was so painful when I didn't hear from him is because my Dad would be so great and wonderful, and we'd be so connected, then he'd disappear without warning and without me being able to do anything about it. Then come back and leave, etc. And with Pierre, we had that intense connection – I trusted him emotionally and he split without warning-totally disappeared and died and there was nothing I could do about it. So, Matt and I really connected, then, when he didn't call, I was hit with the fear that I'd be devastated just like with Dad,

72

Pierre, and Kent. I decided to be willing to work through that fear, hold my power in my center and create a new experience.

September 2004

"I listened to Peter Gabriel's "Digging in the Dirt" on the way to my therapy session with Darcy. He moves me the same way that the Metallica *S&M* album does. So, Darcy was so great. We talked about the excruciating, breathtaking – (literally) pain I felt from Saturday through Tuesday night. It's not really about Matt. His not calling has triggered the pain inside my body from Dad, then my first boyfriend Greg, then Pierre, then Kent. Dad at the core though, starting with his leaving when I was four years old. Darcy talked about how emotional pain becomes physical pain stored in my body – it is a physiological thing – we store painful and other experiences within our body. So when I feel fear, or the pain – I can breathe into the pain – or tightness in my chest, and breathe it out to release it. I can literally stretch my body and breathe through it to let it go. She described pain in my body as sort of a spine with vertebrae and how when I breathe through the pain – stretch through it and be aware and release it, the vertebrae (pain) unhooks from the spine (me) and disappears. When I feel the pain, get afraid, and for example, smoke or eat, I add little vertebrae of more pain into my body. (reminds me of the pain body in *The Power of Now*) Not only that, but that smoking and eating could be an affirmation to the Universe that I am reacting to fear as if the present experience with Matt is the past (with Greg, Kent, Dad, Pierre). That's powerful. Darcy asked if I was ready to release the pain (from Dad) – the fear of abandonment. I didn't answer right away. What

73

would that be like? My body would be a clear channel – no blocks, at least not this huge chunk in my chest. To breathe and stretch through the fear or pain instead of add to it with food or cigarettes. I said I was ready."

* * * * *

"The past three days have been quite an experience. I feel like I started giving birth through my chest Friday afternoon till last night. The past month has been so emotionally and physically stimulating that it will be hard to describe in words but I want to try. It started, July 19th, the day I turned 30. Since that day I have cried from my guts and chest off and on. The feeling was as if I was entering a new world – a birth of some sort. I had a knowing that I was entering a world of new being and blissful experiences, and I have. Running has been a big part of that experience. I felt a new sense of confidence and purpose. I felt good in my body. Going out with Matt was a new experience with a man for me because I felt so comfortable and assured. It was amazingly stimulating and peaceful at the same time. I felt different with him than with anyone else. I'm not sure why, maybe because his charisma was so damn engaging. He captivated my attention like no one else. Then the confusion began, which ended last night in devastating bafflement. A month or two before I met him, I felt more peace and bliss that I ever even imagined was possible. After I met him I've not felt it as much. I have felt excruciating agony. He has been the catalyst in triggering the core feelings of abandonment and helplessness from Dad, then Pierre, and Kent (and others on a smaller scale). I have, in the past week or two, sobbed from my guts and chest like I never have before. The only time that even comes close is when Greg broke up with me at 19. This has been worse. I have felt pain at such intensity that it literally took my breath away. I believe that Matt was a gift because he triggered these chunks of pain in my body – at a cellular level – and I have been releasing them the past two weeks. I really feel like I had labor pains in my chest on Friday and gave birth last night. This experience has turned me inside out. Hemorrhaging this pain. So Friday when I heard that Matt had been back in LA since Tuesday, it started – because he had been back and hadn't called. I felt the devastating, baffling, hot/cold abandonment that's been living inside me for 25 years. I came home from meeting up with friends at the Key Club, sat on the floor, breathed and cried. I didn't smoke (till later Fri night)-that's a miracle. I let myself feel it. I called Darcy and we had a 30 minute phone session – after that I felt more peaceful and centered. Another strange piece of this is that while crying this pain out, I have continued to feel centered and grounded to a certain extent – a knowing that what was happening was positive and healing. So Friday I can say was one of the best, most healing days of my life. It was as if a chunk of pain was released through breathing and crying, and then I ran and it was amazing. I was on a serene high. After my run I got the best massage I've ever had.

The next day I felt the sadness come back because Matt still hadn't called. I felt it coming and I couldn't go to sleep. Got up and drove to work and just sobbed. Peter Gabriel singing "Don't Give Up" was killing me. I felt such anger at Matt, really the situation of having felt such a connection with other men in my life, who, without warning all of a sudden disappeared. I was left feeling helpless and baffled. I smoked all through work. I cried so hard driving home on PCH that I had to pull over because I couldn't see. Got a dress out of the trunk to wipe my eyes and drove back to West Hollywood. I drove up to Pierre's house and SOBBED. When I drove down the hill back to Franklin I stopped crying and a peace came over me. I felt exhausted, still sad, and hungry. Got a burrito at Baja Fresh, went home and went sound to sleep. I slept like a baby. Woke up this morning feeling peaceful."

The next night at work, I had a breakthrough talking with my coworker Eric. I told him how proud I was of myself for declining Matt's invitation to go running again. I was proud that I closed the door of opportunity to seeing him again. I told him that Matt's attention was nice and felt great but it wasn't real or genuine. I didn't feel full anymore after seeing him. As I ate my M&Ms, Eric asked me why I was eating them and I told him it felt comforting. We talked about eating chocolate when I wanted love, comfort and attention. I then had a revelation about men and chocolate. I saw that bingeing on chocolate was like going out with Matt. They both felt great in the moment and got me a bit high. And they both were also not the real thing. They were both knock offs of the real thing for me. Matt wasn't a true love. Chocolate is not real sweetness, it's been toxic for me. I admitted that I wanted real sweetness and real love. I thought about how eating natural, healthy sweetness, can be symbolic of my statement to the Universe that I'm over the knock offs, that I'm now accepting only the real thing.

*****

76

The more I discarded what I didn't want, what I did want had the space to surface. I began to be pulled toward what I was really craving, instead of food. I felt excited discovering there was a whole world of yummy possibilities. Louise Hay's book *You Can Heal Your Life*, introduced me to the idea of thinking big. She affirmed being a beneficial presence on the planet and making a positive impact on a global level. Norman Vincent Peale, in his book *The Power of Positive Thinking,* tells the story of his friend Harlowe Andrews, who believed that the trouble with most prayers is that they aren't big enough. Andrews said "To get anywhere with faith, learn to pray big prayers". Peale sites Matthew 9:29 from the Bible as saying, "According to your faith, be it unto you". At this point, the idea of being a positive influence in people's lives on a large scale was a "pie in the sky" wish. I had no confidence in my ability to be a healing force on a "grand scale", but spiritual giants whose books I read planted the seed of possibility in my mind that I could live beyond my expectations of myself. Planting the seeds of possibility became another discipline is HOW I became free from compulsive eating.

I was clear that just trying not to think about eating did not stop me from thinking about eating. I had to change my focus from what I didn't want to what I did want. When I asked myself in November of 2004 what I wanted most out of life, this was my answer:

"1)Peace of mind – acute clarity in reading people, knowing what they need and giving them love, compassion, light, being an example of living bliss. I want to be in the flow of universal power and direction. I want to exude love to everything and everyone. I want to live free of my mind and body – as the free spirit that I am. I want to experience bliss and wonder every day in all that I do, to my core - without blocks. Ecstasy.

2) Children: I think I'll want some if I fall in love and get married. It's hard to see it right now.

3) Peers: having fun with friends. Creative, expressive, funny, eccentric friends who are adventurous and love life, who are spiritually connected and have a positive influence on me bettering myself.

4) Parents: to show them more love, to be able to buy plane tickets to see them more and buy Mom things.

5) Friends: I want to be a ball of love and glitter to my friends. I want to be someone my friends feel uplifted by and loved when they're with me. I want to inspire my friends and be inspired. I want to continue meeting new higher energy people with magic who are movin' and shakin'. I want to take my friends to new places, physically and spiritually and I want to be taken to new places physically and spiritually.

6) Professional relationships: I want to be loved, respected and needed professionally. I want to be clear and concise in my negotiations. I want work to run smoothly. I want to give love, light and inspiration. I want to be a pleasure to work with.

7) Personal accomplishments: I want to use my voice to spread love and inspiration to people on a grand scale. I want the universe to feel sparkly and loved by me and know that it's God and they have access to the same Power. I want to build my self esteem by treating my body with

the healthiest food, exercise, meditation, right action and positive self -
talk and be an example to those with lower self- esteem. I want to be kind
and loving to all. I want to see how much love I can give myself and other
people each day. I want to spread a healing vibe on a grand scale because
as they say, "shoot for the stars". I'm willing to dream big. Why not?!

8) I want to help people connect with God. I want to be a beam of
God's light. I want to tap into the bliss."

I knew this was an order only God could fill. I needed him to help me
be my "dream me". I still had a lot of gunk that was blocking my bliss. I
prayed:

God,

Please help me. I need your power to suck out the self- centeredness
that blocks me from you and others. I want to be fully charged up by you
to radiate love; not sucking light from the world but radiating it out.
Please rearrange me as I sleep tonight.

*****

For the first time in my life, I spent Thanksgiving of 2004 alone. I ran
up Runyon Canyon and cried all the way up and a lot of the way down. It
actually felt good. I had been losing my breath out of nowhere and crying
from my guts all day. I was wistfully reminiscent of the breathtaking pain
a few months earlier with the Matt upheaval. I sort of missed feeling so
alive. That's what it was... I just felt so alive.

I was reminded again that the pain in being fully alive actually felt better than the pain in trying to avoid it. I was becoming convinced. I knew that being fully alive was the only way I could be the "dream me" living the life I said I wanted.

My therapist, Darcy, not only helped me release 25 years of buried pain with men, but she let me discover for myself that I had some of the same qualities that I found objectionable in the men who had hurt me the most. I had often felt like a victim but I realized that I had sometimes used men like a drug. I was self- seeking in that I saw them as a source for a rush. When they didn't call when I wanted them to call, I'd get angry because I needed a fix. Darcy reminded me that whenever someone is in active addiction they will choose the drug over the relationship. Clearly, I was smoking and fixing on sugar. I always described the men I was attracted to as being emotionally unavailable. Guess who else was emotionally unavailable? ME! I was floored. I was the one who wasn't fully showing up mentally, emotionally and spiritually because of my addictions! I was also often the taker in my relationships because I wasn't filling up from the Source (the term she used for God).

Darcy told me that I could fill up on true love from the Source through meditation. Once again, desperation was a great motivator and I was willing to try it. I tried meditation in the past but my head was so loud I couldn't sit still more than five minutes. I was relieved when she said I could fill up by connecting with nature. I set an intention to use meditation as a "fix". I asked the Universe to reveal itself to me and told the Universe that I wanted to have an intimate relationship with it. It made sense that I must get love from the Source or I would continue to seek and demand it from sugar and men. The next day I experienced meditation through soaking up the sun as I watched it glisten on the ocean. I felt, for the first time, that I needed nothing from human beings.

*****

In the beginning it was so difficult to stay connected with my spiritual experiences. It often felt like someone would just come along and pull the plug, rip it out of the wall without warning. I would be left in the dark wondering what happened. December 4th was one of those days:

"I just quit crying. After days of holding it in, I finally broke down. I have felt, since last night, separated from the love and magic energy of the Universe. I felt tonight like I was being pulled into to the black tunnel of death away from all the love I've ever felt from people, music, men, parents, things. I've felt that my life was as big as a pinprick all in 24 hours. I felt like I was outside of life looking at all the love between people and I couldn't step into the love. Paralyzed in purgatory. This is the feeling and state of being that I've avoided for years with food and cigarettes and I see why. The illusion of separation is harrowingly convincing. So about 30 minutes ago I looked out the window to a star and talked to God. I'm desperate for the true connection to the source of love because men are not it – food and cigarettes are actually further separation and I don't really feel connected yet but I think something heard me. I hope I can use this night of darkness someday to help other people who feel stuck in a black cell of solitary confinement. Why do I feel so "fucking alone"? I think that's an Iggy Pop song. The star became a fountain of light. Tears poured out of my eyes like a fountain. The thought of laying here in bed again tonight with myself and my thoughts is breathtaking. I believe I'm alone and then eat because I'm desperate to feel even fake love/comfort, even though I know it is further separation. I want false comfort for just a second – then smoke to try to feel a fake connection to something. A rolled piece of paper - to expect a relationship and connection with a rolled piece of paper. I've believed that's all there was for me – fake connections that further separate. False love. I've been having a relationship with pieces of food and rolled pieces of paper. I take from them and they suck me into their black hole. God help me.

I'm so fu##ing afraid that God isn't here. That he won't love me – or let me feel love from Him –or that he'll keep me separated. That he won't pull me out of the black hole of death. That he and everyone I know will just watch me just get sucked into the dark. That I'm alone in the dark. Me without love. Seperated. Am I important enough for God to pull me out of the dark tunnel and fly me to a new world of true love? I want to be born into the light of love. I'm so afraid to be stuck in a sea of darkness, suspended in space alone. God give me new eyes. Take me."

I woke up the next morning at eight am to a chainsaw screaming right outside my window. Unbelievable. Eight am. Before I even opened my eyes I saw the blade cut the man's head off. Being woken up too early made me really angry back then. I decided to get up and go for a run. As I walked out my door towards Doheny, I set an intention to have a personal experience with nature. I liked the idea that I could use running as a way to meditate and connect with nature. It beat sitting still trying not to think. What happened that day was the beginning of trippy out of body (and perhaps out of my mind) experiences.

As I ran towards Sunset, I saw myself massaging the Earth – I imagined that it probably felt like finger tips on a person's shoulders. I also saw myself come out of water slaloming, then flying through the air as I listened to Jane's Addiction "Ocean Size". Running up Maple, I saw myself fly low through the trees. They're all in a row and it seemed like the lowest branches to the ground are all at the same level. Running with music took me different places.

I had found a new power outlet in which to connect. The surge felt electric! During my run the next day I was a blood cell running through the veins of the Universe to the heart (of the source of power/love) at the top of the hill. The heart hugged me with its contraction as I reached the top and released me down the hill, charged for my day.

In experiencing this new magical feeling of love, my desire to spread it exploded. First I knew that I needed to be a full expression of it. I set an intention and prayed once again "I want to feel God sparkling through my body. I want to be spiritually orgasmic. I want to be in a love affair with the Universe. I want to feel the cosmos connect and touch my body."

*****

I have to admit, I hadn't ever really listened to the Sex Pistols until I met Steve Jones in West Hollywood. One of my friends was a long time friend of his and I was immediately charmed by his crass since of humor.

Steve and I became friends and one Sunday afternoon he invited me up to his house in Beverly Hills to go swimming. Oh God. I hadn't worn a swim suit in two years and I was still a bit chunky, but I couldn't decline his invitation. This was an opportunity to step outside of my negative body image box that my eating disorder kept me trapped in so often. I was tired of my struggle with food and my weight keeping me from doing fun things with fun people.

Although insecure, I felt surprisingly comfortable around him in my "imperfect" body. Maybe it was his punk rock "f##k what anyone thinks" attitude that rubbed off on me. After lying by his pool listening to Lou Reed, we went inside where he laid me down on his sofa, saying he wanted to take a nap. "Oh, here we go", I thought. "Of course he didn't want me to come over just to swim." He gently placed a pillow under my head and tucked me in with a blanket and said, "I'm going to be in my bedroom, wake me up before you leave." And walked out! Huh? What? Wait, he didn't' want …?" I laid there a bit stunned. Not because I thought I was irresistible, but he was a "Sex Pistol", notorious for playing women as aggressively as he played guitar. I experienced a disarming side of Steve that I suspected many girls hadn't. I was pleasantly surprised by the respect he showed me that Sunday afternoon and I, in turn, gained respect for him beyond his raw talent as an iconic guitar player.

Our friendship continued and on occasion he'd take me to Sushi Ko up Beverly Glen Blvd at Mulholland Drive for a late Friday night dinner. I had never gone out to dinner with someone who showed such total disregard for social graces. And I hadn't laughed so hard since the night Pierre dropped his pants at Matsuhisa. I'll never forget sitting across from Steve one night in his pink t-shirt with a fat pig on the front, shoving a handful of raw fish in his mouth. He belched so loudly, and I was laughing so hard that people were staring. He is a riot! Whereas I might have been offended by another man's shocking debauchery, Jonesy could get away with all kinds of raucous misbehavior. I ran into him at a club a few weeks later and after we hugged and said hello, he stuck his hand down his pants, pulled out his snake and hissed it at me! Oh my God! He was rude and mischievous and I loved him. Despite his infamous reputation with women, he proved to be harmless with me.

I had a lot of fun with him, especially playing name that tune in his living room. He would play a few notes of songs from artists like The Who and David Bowie. I was proud of myself that I named most of the tunes correctly and I really wanted to impress him with my recognition of good music. Listening to music at another friend's house earlier in the year, I heard "Beside You" for the first time. I loved the song, put it on repeat and asked my friend who the artist was. He said it was Iggy Pop with Steve Jones on guitar. Of course I liked the song! So back at Steve's house playing name that tune, he played the first notes of "Beside You". I named it right away and told him how much I liked his guitar on the song. He looked surprised when I said that because he actually had no recollection of recording the song with Iggy. Ha! He said it must have been during his black out "partying days".

Have you heard the saying "Watch out what you pray for, you just might get it?" I felt like Christopher Lloyd's character "Doc" in *Back to the*

85

Future when he touches the ball of electricity. The next day was Monday December 27. I was drying my hair thinking about giving Jonesy the book, "Embraced by the Light" by Bettie Eadie. I imagined myself saying to him "I have something for you". As I saw myself say that, my phone blinged a text message and it was Jonesy saying "I have a gift for you". He was writing that to me as I was seeing myself say that to him. That really freaked me out but in a comforting way that confirms that there is a connection beyond what is tangible.

During this time he was doing his daily radio show called "Jonesy's Jukebox" on LA's Indie 103.1. (I think it now airs on Sundays on LA's KROQ) Not only did he play great music, but he charmed listeners with his eccentric sense of humor and random, live acoustic playing and singing. I couldn't get enough of him and neither could listeners. Ratings went through the roof. I laughed every time I tuned in.

Seeing Steve around was a bright spot in an often dark time in my life. He provided much needed comic relief for the pressure of taking myself too seriously. Jonesy's attention challenged my perception that men were only interested in super skinny model – type girls. I'm grateful our friendship continued (after we became friendly....).

*****

What goes up must come down. Gravity is a bitch. 2005 got off to a rough start for me. I went to hear the band "Camp Freddy" play at the Key Club by myself and felt alone even though I knew a lot of people there. I met a few guys who were trying to get me to have a drink with them. They gave me a Jack and Coke, my old favorite, and it smelled really good. I quickly set it down on the bar. It had been a tough week. A few nights before, I binged at work, snuck down to the pool house, threw up, and the blood vessels around my eyes burst. It scared me. The next night I found out that Jason, a friend I had gone out with a few times, OD'd and died. That was shocking to me. I was dumbfounded and just so sad. During our short six month friendship, he showed me that there were good looking, fun, sober guys who respected women. He said he thought I looked hot one night when I was wearing sweats. That meant a lot to me because it was the first time a guy told me I was sexy without being all dressed up. I couldn't believe he was dead. It just so happened that I changed my phone number the day he died. I called his phone one last time to hear his voice. The last time I saw him was a few weeks before he overdosed. He called to me from across the parking lot, ran over, picked me up and spun me around. We hugged and he said we had to do something soon. He told me to call him and I said I would. I didn't.

So I returned to Runyon Canyon to process another chunk of pain. As I hiked up to Mulholland, I was obsessing about eating brownies when a piece of bright royal blue light on a house flashed across my line of sight. The blue from the house shot into my eyes and flowed down through my body cleansing me. THAT was trippy!

*****

I believe that what you focus on grows and ever since I recovered from my leg surgeries, I learned not to take the simple things for granted. I love making gratitude lists to God and to remind myself that I have an abundance of gifts in my life. A gratitude list would often include: the ability to walk, run, get out of bed, use my hands and fingers, leave my house whenever I please, use the phone, buy healthy food and see the ocean. I was particularly grateful for noticing the trees' leaves looking glossy and almost wet. It's the "little" things that make a big difference.

A coworker and I were walking into work one morning commenting on how beautiful the weather was and I said, "Look at that ocean sparkling at us!" It was then that I realized, I *am* having a personally intimate relationship with the Universe. Gratitude washed over me once again.

I was definitely connecting with the universe and now the lines of separation between me and people "not like me" began to dissolve. On my run through Beverly Hills one day, I had a really fantastic experience. I was running towards some workmen sitting on the sidewalk eating lunch on Elevado Drive. I saw them looking at me and my first reaction was resentment and judgment. But instead of being angry that they might be looking dirty at me, I sent them love and light. The way it happened was what was so cool. Like Spiderman shoots webs out of his wrists, light – like fireworks- shot out of my shoulder and showered them with sparkles. Then rose petals flew out of the top of my head like a fountain – they were pink. It felt really good giving those workmen love.

I also experienced unity with the clients at Renaissance who paid up to $50,000 a month for rehab. I already learned that alcoholism and addiction affect every race, men and women of all ages, "from Yale to jail". No one is immune. But I did feel like these wealthy people had a separating advantage of financial security, which I didn't have. I knew wealthy people all my life and saw that some of them suffered mentally and emotionally worse than people who were poor. What became clear to me is that material wealth can be a burden. The more you have, the more you can lose. The fear of financial insecurity can trample someone with millions in the bank. I wasn't as financially secure as some but I didn't have to have a *fear* of financial insecurity. Working with ultra wealthy clients affirmed the fact that the appearance of a full life is not evidence of a full heart. These people's hearts were broken by alcoholism and addiction. A few of them committed suicide; some continued a slow suicide with drugs and alcohol and some recovered in sobriety.

Similarly, but on a less dramatic scale, I imagine my life in LA appeared to some as being charmed and fabulous. That is true to an extent. The circumstances of my life: my living arrangements, cool people I met, and fun places I went were at times, charmed and fabulous, *and* I was mentally and emotionally tortured a lot of the time by compulsive eating. Pain is relative. Judging someone else's pain in relation to their outside circumstances, I learned, can separate me from my own healing.

*****

The more I focused on having an intimate relationship with the Universe, the more we connected. I set an intention to give the Earth some love on my hike up Runyon Canyon. It had allowed me to process so much pain on its back that I wanted to reciprocate. As I was walking up to the tippy top, my heels seemed to have springs on them and each time I took a step, my springy heel sent a vibration – a ripple effect – of love to

89

the center of the Earth and out. It was pretty cool. In my spirit of giving back that day, I was given another gift which led me further into freedom.

I had just read the section of Wayne Dyer's *Power of Intention* where he talks about imagination. It was revealed to me on my hike that I could use my "trips" to create a superhero character. I could pretend to have her power when I doubted my own. Her name would be Goldie.

*****

I continued to identify the negative beliefs that were creating anxiety and discomfort. I was uncovering my bellyful of bliss slowly but surely. I had figured out that my sleep hang ups did not stem from my own beliefs. I picked up someone else's negative beliefs about sleep as a child. I got through a day at work being really tired but without bingeing by thinking about how Goldie would get through it. I remember crossing my fingers while a psychologist hypnotized me a few months earlier in an unsuccessful attempt to stop bingeing. So I tried crossing my fingers again and pretended that I was Goldie. That worked.

On my way home I made a profound parallel between food, men and love. It became clear to me that when I binge, I stuff myself full of sugary sweets, as if I might never get it again. It scared me to eat just a moderate amount, especially at night. A normal dinner never felt like enough. I saw that it was attached to my Dad being so present in my life, then disappearing and not knowing if he was coming back. It was a similar dynamic with food. I stuff myself when I can get it because I want to fill up before it disappears. I felt a similar intense connection with certain

90

men in my life. After Pierre died and Kent disappeared, those feelings were really triggered. So the cycle was to fill up with a binge then deprive myself. After this deeper awareness, I had a whole new perception and comfort level with eating. *I found myself not wanting or needing to eat too much at one time because the food/love isn't going anywhere!* In my gut, I knew that the food/love would be waiting for me in the morning so I didn't need to overeat at night! It's as if it's waiting for me on my bedside table as I sleep. That image had never occurred to me before.

I've heard many people refer to personal growth as "peeling the layers of the onion". When you peel the layers of an onion, you just get more onion. I think of my path to freedom like peeling the layers of an artichoke. As long as I keep peeling, I'll get to the heart. I had been peeling away the layers of my limited beliefs for a few months when I uncovered the heart and described it in March 2005. This is what happened:

"Yesterday should go down in history for personal/spiritual growth. The fact that I've been physically really tired for a week and I haven't mentally or emotionally collapsed is still shocking. Yesterday morning after I wrote, I tried to go back to sleep and couldn't so I decided I'd go about my day as if I wasn't tired at all. That's a foreign concept for me. Being tired is the daddy of my feeling helpless, powerless, at the mercy of something I can't control or change – which are the exact feelings which exploded at 16 when Dad left again. So I ran errands, hiked at Runyon Canyon, started to feel a little hungry, anxious and alone. I didn't know how I'd get through the rest of the day without eating – or with these

91

emotions because I didn't really know what to do with myself. I felt so uninspired and SAD. I rushed to the yogurt store – ate yogurt and a cookie and wanted to eat another one. I felt like I had to, but I opened my mind a little tiny bit to what I could do instead because I'm now aware that that anxious feeling is just wanting love – being afraid I'm not gunna get it – or it's gunna go away. It's also the feeling of being frozen and stuck and not being able to express it-or admit it-or being afraid to say, "I'm so sad" – to just dramatically surrender to it. I ended up seeing myself get dramatic and throw a fit. It feels empowering and so great! I think babies and kids really have something because they cry and throw a fit when they don't feel right to express and release that energy and then they're over it and go play or go to sleep.

A friend called and I told her I was sad and tired. I told her the truth instead of pretending that I was "fine." I started to feel a little relief – like I might have a little power – or choices/options. I was experimenting with not overeating because I'm learning that there's always more – an abundance at my fingertips when I need it. Love doesn't just disappear without warning like some men in my life. I'm feeling love inside me that must be God. This is massive awareness for me. I release tears of gratitude and let them flow down my face. All day long I felt like the only way to be satisfied would be to eat until I got in bed. I didn't. I can hardly believe it. Miraculous."

The next negative belief to bubble up to the surface was about feeling physically sick. For years I was afraid of feeling sick because being sick meant being alone, weak, disconnected and depressed. I obviously spent many years resisting those feelings! Joy and sickness had not coexisted for me yet. I remember one of the first times I actually enjoyed a sick day. Instead of resisting the feelings, I dramatically fell into the sickness. I completely surrendered to it. I lay in bed like a normal person without guilt, watched TV, and allowed myself to be sick. It was magic. I took a lot of deep breaths. I didn't want to eat to try to make myself feel better. The fear about being sick and feeling helpless and vulnerable was about a three out of ten when before it was always a nine.

The fear of being sick was removed that day and what I found buried underneath was sparkling treasure. I took advantage of my sick day at home and wrote what my intuition was revealing about new thought patterns, my mind/body connection, more negative beliefs to be replaced, and what more I was truly craving. Without muting my inner voice with food, I could hear my life calling loud and clear. Without burying my bliss, I uncovered it and let it all out on paper:

Old Beliefs:

1) Eating is the only way to comfort myself or release anxiety, or feel full. I have no other ways of getting comfort, or releasing anxiety, or expressing sadness, fear or anger.

2) My options are limited and I'm pretty much helpless.

3) I have to binge when I feel fear, sadness or emptiness because it might disappear and then I'll be forever alone, sad, afraid with no

93

solution. Seeing eating as the only option to change my feelings, not believing that I can express my feelings or that there's power in expression.

4) I can't be effortlessly thin, that I'll have to feel empty to be thin. I have to stay small, confined, powerless, motionless and stifled. I'm unable to express myself at all, especially in a creative way.

5) I need someone else to make up for money I can't make on my own. I can't BUY a home and make it mine, maybe a man will, but it won't really be mine. That I don't have the power or freedom to choose BIG and fun and influential jobs. Old belief that making money, source of income is unstable, inconsistent, weak, and could disappear at any moment

6) I'm at the mercy of an authority who can keep me under someone else's roof, who can keep me small and limited in an uncreative, subordinate, unfulfilling job.

7) There's an authority over me who is controlling the love, money, freedom and security

8) The only consistent, reliable, dependable relationship/thing is FOOD!

New Beliefs:

1.) I fill myself up with deep breaths.

2.) I fill myself up with beautiful sights.

3.) I fill myself up with mesmerizing sounds.

4.) I release anxiety by running and exercise.

5.) I identify feelings of anger and physically express the anger through kicking, hitting, screaming – throwing a fit!

6.) I use my power to take positive actions – going outside, making phone calls.

7.) I have many sources of abundant income.

8.) I have the power to create.

9.) I have the power and freedom of choice in how I make money.

10.) Abundance – creativity (choices) and money flows easily and consistently to me.

11.) I am the source of financial security in my life.

12.) I have the power of thinking and creating projects to give love and light and make enough money to support myself comfortably.

13.) I am a powerful – choice making woman who has freedom. I am not stuck and limited in someone else's home. I have the power and creativity and freedom of choice to make my life on my own and employ other people.

14.) I determine the flow of love, money, peace and energy in my life.

15.) I am the creator of love, money, freedom and security. I have the power of choice to tap into the Universe's love and abundance.

16.) My power, creativity and freedom of choice are dependable, reliable, consistent and always INSIDE of me – it lives in my center!

17.) I am independent and live from abundance, flexibility and freedom.

My Inspiration Mantra:

What do I want out of my life?

1) I want to express unlimited creativity with love and light to individuals on a global level. I want to use my voice to inspire people – to move energy around in people, to give them chills like David Bowie and Metallica and Moulin Rouge have given me. I want to show and teach people – especially children – how to choose love in thoughts and action every day in their lives and to make inspiring people fun – like through Goldie – and loving the Earth and taking care of it and appreciating it on a global level. I want to give love on a grand scale. I want to receive love and feel love from the Universe – and from people, and a man who I love.

2) I want freedom of choice in my personal daily life in how I meet my needs. I want to use my power positively and have an always open mind.

3) I want to sing, love, feel free and powerful and clear. I want to write stories to teach people and help heal the Earth.

4) I want to own my own home before I get married. I want to travel and buy my brother and Mom and Dad lots of stuff and transfer money into their account. I want to have them visit me in my home and take them places and pay for whatever we do.

What inspires me?

1) Music-creative sound expression

2) Love, expressions of love, kindness

3) Imagination

4) Intuitive "knowing" in the center of my being – spiritual connections with others

5) Sharing love and fun with others

6) Running

Short Term Daily Goals:

1)   To honor my body – eat when I'm hungry and stop when full

2) Be true to my emotions – express anger physically and say it out loud – admit it! Express fear out loud and choose one of many solutions – be open- minded to many solutions.

3) Embrace freedom of expression – with my own feelings and creatively with my thoughts and imagination

4) Explore and express my imagination

5) Meditate each day/breathe deeply

6) Share my love, light and laughter to others

7) Sing – always listen to music I love and sing, sing, sing!

Affirmations:

1) I have the power of choice to get what I need.

2) I am free to choose from many sources of love.

3) I am dramatically expressive.

4) I am free to move and change my outside circumstances anytime I wish.

5) I am free to verbally admit and express anger, fear, sadness and loneliness and I can be dramatic about it.

6) I am the authority figure/boss in my life.

7) I determine where I live, where I go, what I do and when.

8) I have the source of choices and power inside me.

9) Love, comfort and relief are waiting for me.

10) I am free to get love and comfort whenever I need it.

11) Love, comfort and power are inside me always whenever I need it. ALWAYS.

12) My creativity and imagination flows at a peaceful, manageable pace. I organize my running "trips" and give them back to the Universe in the form of entertainment/ healing, and I earn money, forever, from many different sources.

13) I know the next step to take to bring my projects to the world and get paid for them.

14) I want to feel God (good), magic inside me. Universal energy and power flows through my body, cleansing the blocks inside me.

15) I choose to see God everyday– in the magic on my way to work and home, in the faces of the clients, and in humor.

16) I choose to dramatically express myself today verbally and make a powerful choice to get my needs met. I am free to move and express power.

17) I look at other people and see them feeling loved, hugged, comforted, and at peace in their minds.

In looking inside my body with curiosity instead of judgment I see:

1) Heart – it's flowing but sad, stingy, smushed, tense, shameful feelings in my chest

2) Kidneys: pain, hard, blocked lower back, sharp, searing

3) Lungs: weak energy – holding my breath, flowing but weak

4) Intestines: dirty, blocked, shame, heavy, dark energy flows but it's choppy, sometimes stuck – toxic

5) Stomach: dark, food – energy gets stuck here, weak, it doesn't feel strong or vigorous and vibrant. It feels unbalanced, not flowing

6) Glutes: shame, naked, embarrassed, hard, energy gets stuck here and no new energy even flows here, frozen

7) Quadriceps – thighs: angry, defeat, heavy, dark

8) Arms: light and sort of weak, but energy flows

9) Back and Shoulders: energy stuck but only in small pieces, the energy moves but its pain, no shame

10) Back: lower – pain to bend over, rigid, energy stops at my butt

11) Inner thighs: very sensitive and weak, shame, no energy goes there

When I asked myself why energy was blocked, I knew it was because I still sometimes felt trapped and alone. It seemed like, despite my efforts to release the pain of the past, I was still stuck.

I know that this energy originated in 11th grade when Dad moved back home after leaving for the third time. I felt helpless and powerless, like my feelings didn't really matter. I felt like my security was at the mercy of his instability. When he left, part of me felt sad but a bigger part of me felt relieved that he took the tension with him. Rage erupted from deep inside me when he came back. I felt like I was on fire and no one would look – or see. I felt alone and was afraid I'd get in trouble if I expressed my anger. My rage wouldn't change the circumstances. I was trapped in it and powerless over it. No one heard me. My spirit was stuffed down even more. I felt shame and kept my anger about certain things a secret.

My Senior year of high school I was isolated and trapped in my house. My After Care Plan from rehab prohibited social activities that were without adult supervision. I felt separated from my senior class. I couldn't do anything about it. I had no power against my parents or my doctors from rehab. NO FREEDOM. All I could do to treat my feelings and quiet my head was binge, purge and smoke. My rage blazed quietly inside.

What's important is not to focus on painful memories from the past, but to identify where your beliefs began so that you can separate from them. I appreciate every effort my parents made to take care of me. They were trying to stop me from self- destructing with alcohol. In retrospect, I see that living with me was no picnic. I was in a lot of pain, but so were my parents. My selfish behavior played a big part in how they dealt with my rebellion. My anger at my parents has dissolved into compassion. They used their parenting tools with all the love they had, they were just sometimes the wrong tools. The origin of my self destructive coping mechanisms is not my parent's fault. Another person could have used my circumstances to promote power and positivity. My Dad and I have healed our relationship and my mom and I have become best friends. The pain and rage that once burned inside me has turned into the bliss that blows my mind today.

*****

I managed to lose a few pounds using the disciplines I had discovered so far. Forgiving myself for bingeing and all the reasons I hated myself allowed self love and love from others to seep through. It seemed like, the less I compulsively ate, the more love I allowed in my life. During this (short) period of weight loss I met Jason. Jason was a 6'4 Ben Affleck look-a-like whose charisma and dynamic presence stopped me in my tracks. I hadn't been in a relationship, besides a few dates, in three years and I was ready to have some fun! I don't know if he was attracted to me because I looked sexier or because I felt sexier. I know now that feeling confident and comfortable in my skin is always more attractive than being thin and insecure. I quickly experienced the difference between the LA dating scene (that my girlfriends complained about) and the Memphis dating scene. Dating in LA often meant "hooking up", or last minute "meet ups" for a night out. Our first "meet up" involved me picking him up at his friend "Matty's" house. I wasn't accustomed to picking up a guy for a date but, ok. I followed the directions he gave me up the hill north of Sunset into Beverly Hills. As I approached the house I thought, "What friend of his lives in this fancy neighborhood?" The stepping stones to the front door were surrounded by some sort of garden pond. When I walked in, I noticed an atrium in the middle of the house. I looked up to see the stars in the sky. "What a cool house", I thought. Jason called to me from the office and when I walked in I saw photos on the wall of Matthew Perry and the cast of the hit TV sitcom "Friends". Oh, that Matthew, of course.

Anyway, after a month or two, it became clear that Jason's plans with his friends always took priority over me. As handsome and fun as he was, casual, inconsistent hangouts didn't feel good to me.

Maybe I was still an old fashioned Southern girl in the sense that I wanted to be courted and treated like a top priority. A phone call for a date a couple of days in advance didn't seem like too much to ask. Well, it was for a lot of guys in LA. The disappointment of feeling like I was on the back burner started to make me sick, literally. I told God when I met Jason that if he was not right for me, just give me a neon sign and I'd stop seeing him before the relationship became too dysfunctional. After being stood up for the second time, I ended up in the Emergency Room at Cedars Sinai. I had been sick with severe migraines, nausea, body aches and fatigue for nine days. The doctors ran all kinds of tests only to find nothing wrong. Sitting in the exam room at two in the morning I thought, "Is it possible that the emotional pain of holding on to this relationship is causing my physical pain?" The nurse came in and offered a spinal tap to test me for meningitis. What? I thought, "Let me break up with Jason for good, let go of him completely and just see if I feel better before you stick a needle in my spine." I politely declined the spinal tap and called Jason the next day. I told him it would be best for me if we didn't see or talk to each other ever again. I hung up the phone and let go absolutely. Can you believe that all of my symptoms subsided within 24 hours? Was that just a coincidence? My intuition says "No". Ignoring my intuitive voice with men or muting it with food created unbearable pain. I was learning........slowly.

*****

In flirting with forgiveness and identifying the roots of my bingeing belief systems, I was able to slow down enough to have my first "IHA Moments". *I*dentifying, *H*onoring, and *A*llowing my thoughts and feelings in the moment became another one of the disciplines in how I became free. Staying present with discomfort proved to be the next key to freedom. Making intentions and visualizing each successful segment of my day helped me to see that it was possible to stay conscious and free from bingeing. A simple belief in possibility became another discipline in how I became free. I had heard about athletes using mental preparation to help win races, so in my spirit of being willing to try anything, (and desperation), I imagined the possibility of winning throughout my day and wrote out my visualizations:

March 2005

"Vision for the rest of the day: I see myself eating a healthy – pure energy dinner and drinking tea and writing to express my feelings. I also see getting a coffee from Starbucks later if I want it. I see myself going downstairs at the beach house, turning on the TV and laying on the sofa to relax. I see myself driving home, my stomach feeling a little empty – ready for sleep. I see myself in bed, drifting into a deep sleep.

I'm at the beach house – I'm feeling sad and lonely. This feeling is manageable though. The feeling during, and after a binge is not manageable."

*****

"Today I see myself at peace in the moment, eating a pure energy dinner, going downstairs at the beach house to write and express myself – to face and feel what's going on. I see myself really looking and feeling in my body what's going on with it. I see myself driving home maybe a little insecure and afraid but talking to the Universe and getting in bed with the feelings and if they weren't released, it's ok."

*****

During a run I asked God and made the intention to, with every step, unlock stuck energy in my thighs and butt, and with every breath, to be cleansed and energized. I had an image of a little girl stuck in my thighs and holding on around my leg, frozen. She was too scared to move. I rarely felt anything in my thighs; it was as if they were numb, or asleep. I felt a desire to love my thighs back to life. I wanted to release that little girl and let her go run free. I wanted to feel energy flow through the parts of my body that were blocked.

I was facing more feelings that were buried deep down. What I discovered was simple. I was afraid to feel the on-edge, shaking inside feeling that bubbled up when I didn't stuff it down at dinner. It was like a monster woke up inside me before bed and I could put him to sleep with sugar, or face him and feel the feelings. I could either swallow the loneliness and add to it, or meet the monster and add to my self esteem. I was becoming acutely aware that the food wasn't necessarily bad, but after I took the last bite, I was going to feel the same as when I started eating. The food was not changing my feelings for the better. I was starting to *know* that deeper into my guts.

105

*****

Aside from working in one of the most beautiful spots on the Southern California coast, one of the biggest perks of my job at Renaissance was being surrounded by healing professionals. I learned about the benefits of many alternative therapies from Equine Therapy, Reflexology, Sweat Lodges, and Acupuncture. I was intrigued with Eastern healing but the most influential healer in my life at that time was the Medical Director who was also an Addiction Specialist. He provided medical care to the clients and he also gave fascinating weekly lectures on addiction and the brain. He explained how the pleasure centers in the brain worked and how alcoholics and addicts have a broken pleasure center as a result of substance abuse. Dr. Thomas said that just as you put a cast on a broken arm, certain non-narcotic, non-addictive psychiatric medication can serve as a cast to help heal the brain.

I had been on an emotional and mental roller coaster for years. After two days of bingeing, purging, and calling in sick to work, I got in the bathtub. It was 1:30 in the morning and I was exhausted, but couldn't sleep.

I asked God to just take me.

I went to work the next morning and was on the verge of tears all day and everyone noticed. I barely said two words. I couldn't put a smile on and fake it. I had flat-lined.

Dr. Thomas asked how I was doing day and I told him the truth about my mental and emotional turmoil and my eating disorder. I explained

106

that I had been suffering with it for close to thirteen years and felt stable at times but would always fall off an emotional cliff at some point. My inexplicable moods swings had torn me up and worn me out. I explained that some days I felt grounded and out of nowhere I would get swallowed up by a sinkhole. It would then take days to pull myself out of the hole. He prescribed a mood stabilizer that raised the bottom of my depression so that I could climb out easier. It didn't stop me from bingeing but I was able to function with it in a healthier way. Dr. Thomas was an angel in my life. I still suffered but I didn't secretly want to die anymore.

*****

LEARNING HOW TO DISSOLVE THE DESIRE TO EAT

Discovering the disciplines kept my hope for freedom alive after each binge. I had heard that deep and lasting change is a daily practice, not simply a result of learning the answer once. This road to freedom was an inner experience of uncovering my bellyful of bliss. I wouldn't experience consistent freedom until I had discarded everything that was blocking my bliss.

"IHA" Moments

I was beginning to practice *I*dentifying, *H*onoring, and *A*llowing whatever I was feeling in the moment to be as it was, without trying to change it. I told a friend one day that I felt fat. She said that "fat" wasn't a feeling. Brilliant. The feelings were: unattractive, unloved, and alone. I felt afraid of rejection and too weak to change. I needed to feel in control and empowered so that I felt loved, accepted and attractive – to myself. When I overate, I was trying to kill the painful feelings.

I had a new experience. I felt compassion for myself and those feelings, instead of a need to punish myself for having painful feelings. It felt good to think of loving myself through those feelings instead of punishing myself with food. It's like looking at those feelings like a little precious child was having them. I wouldn't hurt a child if she told me she felt unattractive, unloved, and alone. I'd probably hug her and tell her the truth: that she's surrounded by love and she has power to love herself by taking positive, loving actions. I could do that.

May 2005

"I feel a new sense of hope and freedom this morning. And I really need to write. I feel free to honor my body with food when it's hungry and to feel the feelings when it's not hungry. My feelings of the most freedom ever around food were when I'd only eat when my stomach growled and stopped before I was full. So I have permission to not eat today until I get hungry. Thank God. So that's gunna leave a lot of room for feelings.

So I forgive you, Amy, for hurting yourself for having painful feelings. I forgive you for eating when really, you were afraid you were unloved and unattractive. I forgive you for not liking your body. I forgive you for criticizing your body everyday. I forgive you, Amy, for telling yourself that your body isn't good enough. That you're ok, but not good enough to be loved and accepted. I forgive you, Amy, for being too afraid to feel your feelings and eating. I forgive you for eating to punish yourself for feeling unloved, unattractive and helpless. I forgive you, Amy. You are free to feel your feelings and move through them. You are free to love your body. You are free to accept yourself just as you are right now, today. You are free to eat like a normal person, when your stomach needs food. And you are free to not eat if you are not hungry, just like a normal person. I love you and you have a new power and a new freedom today. Congratulations."

I had a breakthrough as a result of an IHA moment at work that left me with a new sense of power, freedom, and peace. I got an opportunity to unlock, release and heal past anger. This is what happened:

I picked roses and put them beside each client's bed. I felt connected picking the roses and it felt great giving love. I ate dinner because I was getting hungry and left some on my plate because I was full. I helped a coworker prepare for the new client and I was very centered, focused, and felt in control. When the clients got back, John (a client) came downstairs and asked who was in his room. The new client had been moved into his room while John was at the Sweat Lodge and he didn't know until he walked in and the new client's things were there. I felt hit with feelings and I can now understand why I had such a strong reaction. I felt so sad and protective of John. I also felt angry at my coworker and whoever else was involved because they didn't let John know that the new client would be in his room when he got back. I went outside and got in touch with what I was feeling and had clarity. It felt like a breakthrough. This situation affected me so much because I have such strong feelings of suddenly being in a painful situation without any warning and feeling trapped, helpless and powerless to change it. Like I was just at the mercy of an authority figure and if I said anything I'd get in trouble. In the past, when I've had a strong reaction to painful feelings, I didn't, right away, give myself the honor of looking deeper to see what I was really feeling and why. Because I did that, my channel remained clear. How profound. I did not judge my reaction or try to numb it, or punish myself for not having "good feelings". I gave myself the dignity of time and energy to see what was really going on. I had respect for my feelings and I was able to talk to John with appropriate boundaries. He talked to my coworker, and he moved to a new room. Because I had love and honor for myself, and my feelings, I was able to get clear and help John not be trapped and angry. I see that lots of anger resulted in me from feeling like I was trapped and helpless time after time, over and over in my life.

With every IHA moment came appreciation and respect for the miracle that is my body. I could feel my body heal every time I honored and allowed it to be without overeating.

May 2005

"Right now, I can honor the heaviness I feel in my body – I can hold it with respect. It has left over energy to use and it's working well. And my brain and my body are communicating. I takes a lot of effort to pause and really listen to my body. It seems like, in listening to and honoring my feelings and my body, I'm gunna feel clear and look better. It makes sense that if I'm not stuffing anger and fear with food, the feelings and the fat will be released. My intention for the day is to listen to and honor my feelings and my body. And I already did that today. At Coffee Bean, I listened to my body and wanted hot instead of iced. And instead of a large vanilla soy latte because I wasn't that empty, I got a medium soy latte without vanilla and it's delicious and I won't feel too full. I'm really catching on and this feels really good.

So about my body and weight: I do trust that when I honor my body – respect it – listen to it – and put food in my stomach only when it asks for it- the weight will just fall off. That's happened before. I am not stuck, helpless, at the mercy of, or powerless over the fear of rejection. I have a choice to honor and accept those feelings and to honor my body so that I will feel better about how I look. I am free to change my body through accepting my feelings and listening to my body. First to listen to it, then accept it, then act appropriately to give it what it needs when it's not food. For example, rest, exercise, pampering. But first and foremost – to listen and not judge or punish when it feels other than great. I do have the power of choice."

I realized that the sadness wasn't about being over weight, it was about rejecting myself for so many years. Punishing myself and rejecting my feelings and my body was what hurt. I knew I needed a connection and I would either get it from food, or from within. I discovered that if I could honor and connect with my feelings and my body first, *then* I could connect with other people at the level I so desire. At that point I was able to go out, twenty pounds overweight, and still feel good about myself. *That* was growth.

111

*****

What's inside this *EMPTINESS*??

"I have a huge chunk of feelings from yesterday and today to identify, honor and allow. Last night I was in the obsession and compulsion. I was afraid to go home and be conscious of the emptiness before I go to sleep. Because I hate the emptiness inside me, I run from it – or numb it – avoid it – smush it – with food. I'm afraid to see the emptiness inside me. It has been with me for years. It has been an enemy for years. I'm afraid if I see it, feel it, allow it to be – it will take control over me – be bigger than me. But – running from it – avoiding, hating, numbing it – that's what gives it power over me. Actually sitting with myself and listening to it and writing what it's saying and allowing it to be there, that gives me the control.

So I can be with that emptiness and describe it, allow it to be, honor it and have compassion for it. I can be in control of it – instead of running from it and going unconscious. That's when it takes over, grows and swallows me and becomes scarier. I have been rejecting a part of me, that empty part of me. And in the rejection and fear it sticks, and grows. Embracing and allowing it to be releases it. So today, now, I feel clear. I feel empowered. I feel like I've moved forward into more control and more clarity. I commit to staying present and connected to myself – my feelings-my body- and tonight I commit to writing two more times today. I commit to feeding my stomach when it asks for food. I do feel a little blocked – some resistance to getting up and getting dressed for work. I'm afraid of judging and rejecting myself. I allow myself to feel resistance. And I allow myself to want to be thinner. I also allow my body to be as it

112

is and I thank it for looking as good as it does. I honor my feelings of hope and excitement."

*****

I always enjoyed going back home to Memphis for a visit but at this point I was heavy and disappointed that I hadn't lost weight. The anxiety that my friends and family would reject me, or silently say I wasn't a success echoed an old voice in my head. I faced the fear of disapproval by reminding myself, "I can feel my feelings until 11:00 tonight." I knew it wasn't about the food, it's about the feelings. One day at a time. I also decided that I cared more about what I thought of myself than what others thought of me. I sat on my throne with my pen and paper and gave myself many IHA moments. I reminded myself to be gentle with myself. I was learning a new way of living. I overate a few times but made it through the trip without bingeing! Amazing! I returned to LA feeling sad and homesick. I binged. I asked myself why I didn't binge in Memphis. What was different? I wrote to discover the missing piece:

"What is it about home that filled in the space that needs to binge, especially after dinner?

At home I felt:

1) a stronger sense of comfort

2) connected to Mom on a deep level – I feel like she's really there for me emotionally, physically, and mentally

3) support and love on a deeper level at home

4) taken care of at home

5) relief from the pressure of working and bills and being alone.

6) the roots of my childhood, my life for 25 years.

That's a lot of positive feelings – vital feelings for health – that I do not feel in LA. How can I feel those feelings here? I've read that I can trigger those feelings in myself because I have them stored in me. So they aren't "living" in Memphis.

I can intend to feel in LA:

1) a stronger sense of comfort here

2) connected to friends and nature on a deeper level

3) I can feel love and support on a deeper level from friends here and from the Universe, the birds, the flowers, the ocean and nature

4) I can feel taken care of from the Universe more – here

5) I can feel relief from the pressure of work and being isolated and alone – here

6) I can feel five year old roots here – and know my roots are growing really deep for many more years here.

7) I intend to feel a sense of relief and comfort at the Beach House at night and look forward to feeling supported, and comforted on the drive home.

My intention for this writing is to create feelings of connectedness, comfort, support, love and relief here in LA:

1) I intend to feel support, connectedness, love, relief, grounded from sources here in LA

2) the excitement of my future here with my soul mate – imagining that he is close to me

3) the excitement and comfort that my career is developing here in LA

4) the excitement and comfort of me taking care of myself financially is here now and is growing

5) the awareness that I will live in my own home I create for myself and knowing I'll have the comfort of my own family here someday

6) the excitement and comfort that I am creating a life where I can go to Memphis more often and still have a home here

I uncovered and discovered the true meaning of the comfort of home. That experience was the beginning of my ability to feel at home anywhere in the world. "Home is where the heart is" was no longer a corny cliché, I was feeling it.

I continued to pray and meditate during my runs with remarkable results. I loved how Wayne Dyer's *Power of Intention* was focusing my thoughts to create new experiences. I spoke the seven faces of intention from his book out loud while running and focused on my breath. I saw myself breathing in abundance and breathing out abundance to every car that passed. I saw the seven faces of intention as my seven chakras. Each face had a different color and they all spun high energy and the color bled into each other to make a kaleidoscope inside my body. I saw violet energy with specs of aqua blue and white. It was sort of cyclical like a tornado moving through my body. I breathed it in and it moved through my body. I exhaled it out to the Universe until I felt chills crawl up my legs and take my breath away. I gasped!

I felt so energized that I didn't want to stop running, so I passed Doheny and continued east on Sunset. As I was approaching the café, Le Petit Four in Sunset Plaza, I noticed an older man sitting at a table on the front patio. Instead of facing the table, his chair was turned west toward the sidewalk. He was sitting by himself, staring in my direction. I felt giddy as he watched me run towards him. "Why is that older.....sexy.... man staring at me?" I looked around and behind me. Is he looking at me? The closer I got, the black sunglasses, ear to ear grin, and receding hairline was unmistakable. Oh. My. God. Jack Nicholson was watching me run up Sunset! (Granted, he wasn't exactly going out of his way to look at me, I was already in his line of sight, but still!) Breathless, I made eye contact, let out some kind of "Oh, Hi!" waved and kept running. I couldn't even believe that I had just run not even a foot away from Jack Nicholson. Now THAT was thrilling. I felt too nervous about running that close to him again on my way home, so I crossed Sunset at the Chateau Marmont. His energy was just electric. I was still zinging! I couldn't even take it! So when I got closer to Sunset Plaza I was glad I'd crossed the street because the paparazzi were doing what they do, swarming, flashing, harassing.

I had worked up a sweat by the time I got home so I went to the pool, lay on my back at the edge and dipped my head into the cool water. It was the best feeling! Then I looked up at the treetops in the sky and felt awe and magic while my body cooled from my head down. It felt like heaven.

*****

I started to imagine what it would feel like to be at my goal weight. I was a little afraid of the sexual energy I'd feel and give off. I was afraid of its power and questioned my ability to control it. I imagined myself feeling comfortable and strong in a thinner body. I knew it was possible to feel in control and grounded in a thin, healthy body.

I met Lisa through a mutual friend and we became good friends right away. She was not just another pretty girl in a hot body, she was the most grounded, level headed friend I'd made so far. She was a lawyer (that makes three of my closest girlfriends, what's up with that?) who also loved to go out and have a good time. She was a great example of being strong, in control and comfortable in a healthy, thin body. All aspects of her life seemed so balanced; emotional and mental stability, physical health, and a strong moral compass. I also admired her strong work ethic. At times, I felt like a hurricane next to her still waters.

I met Billy Duffy, the guitar player of one of my favorite bands, The Cult, when I first moved to LA. Billy was another rough- around- the-edges Brit whose good looks and accent were irresistible. Billy's mischievous sense of humor was magnetic. There's something about cocky, flirtatious, British rock stars that was just intoxicating. (Well, I guess that's a no brainer.) So I invited Billy and Lisa to a party I gave, they hit it off and dated for a minute. Billy invited us to come see his band, The Cult, play and I was so excited! I had only seen them once, in Memphis, when I was fifteen. I had a crush on Billy and Ian Astbury, the singer, as a teenager. If someone had told me back then that I would someday have an invitation from Billy to see his show, I would have jumped right out of my skin. This was going to be so fun, I couldn't wait! I was looking forward to the show for a month but my compulsive eating beat me into a depression so deep that I cancelled on Lisa the day before and missed the show. I had nothing to wear that I would feel comfortable in and just couldn't rally. It was another fun opportunity at my fingertips that compulsive eating stole right out of my hands. It makes me feel so sad thinking about how I isolated and punished myself for not believing I looked good enough. I also know that the physiological effects of pumping massive amounts of sugar into my body in a short period of time caused me to crash into depression and fatigue over and over. Again, I felt like the life I longed for was waiting for me outside my door and I was locked inside with my eating disorder, watching it pass me by.

Lisa made plans for us to meet her friend Matt Sorum, the drummer for Guns N' Roses and later, The Cult, at Swinger's for dinner one night. Swinger's in West Hollywood was where my friends and I seemed to always meet up on our way out or end up on our way home. Right after we joined Matt, Slash walked in and sat down across from me. What?!

118

Matt introduced us and Slash muttered behind his hair, "Hi, I'm Slash." I thought, "Wait, really?! I had no idea, I've just been rocking out to your music most of my life and I can't believe you're sitting across from me right now!" That was definitely a thrilling, surreal moment. But again part of me felt like, because I didn't have the thin body that most men seemed to want, that they didn't even notice me. It's painful to remember how "not good enough" I felt sitting in that booth, just because I was fifteen pounds overweight. Fifteen pounds! From what my head told me, you would think that I was obese. That's the corrosive nature of eating disorders. The loss of perspective blew the reality of my average size body completely out of proportion. Thinking that fifteen pounds separated me from the life I wished for illustrates the insanity of eating disorders. Even when I was rubbing elbows with stars, the dark cloud of compulsive eating kept me in the shadows.

Lisa and I left Swinger's to meet the guys at the Standard Hotel downtown. It was one of those private Hollywood parties with all kinds of famous people. Matt got us in the door and as I was waiting for my Diet Coke at the bar, a stiletto smashed my toe. I looked up, way up, and it was Giselle Bunchen, pushing through the line with Naomi Campbell. (By the way, they are just as stunning in person as they are in magazines.) I never got caught up in the happening Hollywood scene. I knew nothing "magic" happened at those parties where some people thought they *had* to be. Nothing particularly fabulous was going on. The best part of being at the opening of the Standard Hotel was seeing the interesting architecture of the furniture and the view of LA from the downtown rooftop. In the end, those types of parties were a hassle to get into for not much fun. I'd rather go to a concert in a dive bar by myself.

You know what's crazier than me (a far- from- famous, relatively conservative Southern girl) hanging out with rock stars? What's crazier is the way my thoughts about my body determined the amount of fun I allowed in my life. As I've said, I knew women who were heavier than me, who lived their life fully, had fun and loved fiercely. A heavy body is not what was separating me from fun. The cause of my eating disorder lived in my head. When I rejected myself, I rejected the good in my life. The judgment of my thoughts, feelings and body is what separated me from the life I longed for. Allowing my weight to effect my self esteem was tragic. I wouldn't say that I had low self esteem, I really loved parts of myself. I was proud of myself for graduating from college with honors. I loved that I was sober and living with integrity. I loved the adventurous part of me who took a risk and moved to Los Angeles. I also loved that I knew better than to chase fame, money, or prestige. Although I loved attention from men, I knew that no man could save me from my pain. I loved that I knew seeking God was my only hope for deep and lasting freedom and fulfillment. I liked who I was at the core, but I hated my eating disorder and how it held me back from living my life to the fullest. I hated the shame that lurked in the shadows.

*****

My setbacks continued to force me into a deeper search for spiritual satiation. I didn't realize it at the time, but what felt like a step back after a binge, was really a step deeper into freedom.

"I'm tired of my feelings controlling me. I'm really tired of food having power over me. I'm tired of struggling on the roller coaster. I want freedom and peace. I'm tired of running from myself. I'm so tired of thinking "I can't". Every time I consume food or cigarettes it blocks the creativity, love, abundance and peace that I really want. I'm tired of the lies, like I need food when I don't – or – I need a cigarette when I don't, or that food is peace, or love, or comfort, or safety. God, please erase all my negative thinking. A good thing to do would be to write all the positive thoughts to create positive reality:

I want to be excited about a true love experience with the Universe without food and cigarettes blocking it. I want to live clear headed and clear bodied. I want to be brave and strong. I invite an abundance of positive thoughts. "

Writing has always been the best way for me to purge my true feelings. I have to be honest about my negative feelings before I can move forward into the positive. Unedited venting is vital for change. It was only after I emptied the trash in my head that I could focus on positive thoughts. I liked to think about what I was looking forward to. If my present moment was blah, I could get excited about the future, and make lists of what I loved, in the moment. I would look forward to things like feeling hunger and eating a healthy meal, feeling comfort and relaxation when I get in bed at night, getting my hair done and feeling pampered. I also looked forward to running, experiencing God in ways I had not yet, swimming with a thin, healthy body, putting on skinny jeans and looking hot, and successfully giving love to the Universe. Imagining things I loved shifted my energy and my feelings. Since writing those lists years ago I have experienced everything I was looking forward to, and my lists of "loves" are still relevant today. I still think about great outdoor concerts, breathtaking views of LA and the beach, massages, and running. I sometimes feel stuck in the present moment. This exercise was a great way for me to keep the love and inspiration flowing in the midst of perceived stagnation. I could still be sitting at my desk at work, but my experience of the moment had been infused with inspiration.

GOLDIE TO THE RESCUE!

After bingeing again, I decided it was time to deal with that monster again who woke up when it was time for me to go to sleep. In an effort to knock him out with food so I could sleep, I was still awake hours later feeling so bloated that I couldn't even lay down. Experiencing the dark place inside me in bed alone was too scary. I sent Goldie, my inner superhero, into the darkness to discover what it was that I was so afraid of. I pulled out my pen and paper not knowing that I was about to discover the core of the penetrating fear of going to bed fully present at night, with my stomach healthily half empty – or not stuffed. I found the treasure wrapped in creative expression.

"So, the feeling of being half empty in my stomach –or – God forbid– a little hungry - before bed is absolutely terrifying to me. WHY? I'm not exactly sure, but part of it is definitely a trust issue. Because when I imagined what the feelings looked like, this scene became vividly clear. Its night, Goldie is traveling forward on her journey, she approaches a dark ocean. Her choices are – to stay on the stable, solid, known land she's been traveling, or to step into the ocean onto the life boat to take her to a new land – which is unchartered territory. Every night she turns her back in fear and spends the night on the land. But in the back of her mind, her curiosity is growing. She is intrigued with the idea of a new, different, more beautiful place. Every night that she stays on the land, she grows increasingly sad, she doubts herself and the ocean. She's afraid that she'll never get to the other side. She's afraid that she'll be stuck in the middle of the ocean – day after day, night after night – ALONE – and die alone. She imagines boats and planes passing without seeing her. She's helpless and hopeless. She is afraid of the sea creatures. They are poking at her, laughing "what are we gunna do with her?" It's ALL just fear in Goldie's imagination. These fears are keeping her from moving forward.

Seeing the peaceful beauty of the moonlit, sparkling water singing an invitation to her to come in, she gathers up her courage and the life boat appears. She tries to get on with her backpack of binge food but she can't pick it up because it's too heavy. She realizes that even if she got her "security" on the lifeboat, it would sink. She leaves the backpack on the shore, says bye and thanks it for always being there when she believed she needed it.

It's bedtime and it's dark. She climbs on the shaky life boat *in faith* because she's terrified. She feels cold, vulnerable. A storm comes and a bird shields her from the rain with its wings. As she's floating away from the shore she realizes that the ocean and all the life UNDER THE SURFACE – prove to be all loving, friendly, helpful, and giving. Not only that, but the water itself proves to be the most powerful force that holds her. It has a deep comforting voice. Its loving sound vibration is an old trustworthy character who adores her. Goldie falls asleep.

The next morning a momma bird takes her babies to Starbucks to get Goldie's favorite coffee. All the babies in unison order the "soy, no foam, latte with an extra shot of espresso". So they fly the coffee with the utmost care to Goldie's lifeboat. When they land next to Goldie and it doesn't spill they sing, "Hallelujah, Hallelujah, Hallelujah!!!" The singing birds and the smell of coffee woke Goldie out of a deep, transformative sleep. They give the latte to Goldie and the momma bird is proud. Goldie thinks she's dreaming.

She is surprised by the love. Then the under water creatures turn her boat around pointing east so she can see the breathtaking sunrise. The sun's warmth and light envelop her and she feels cuddled by the sunlight. All the fish are celebrating. After she gets her bearings she apologizes for being so afraid of the ocean and its creatures. "How could I have been so wrong?" They tell her they are used to passengers being afraid and always being so pleasantly surprised when they wake in the morning to peace and beauty. Goldie looks surprised and curious – "You mean someone else has traveled on the water alone at night?" She felt so alone in her experience, like no one had the same struggles as she did. The wise ocean replies, "Yes, you must sometimes travel alone – that's one of the rules of faith!"

When Goldie reaches the shore the ocean says goodbye and Goldie cries. The ocean thanks her and is honored and proud that she finally took a ride on it so it could transport her to her new world. She thanks the ocean and asks how she could ever repay it, or give a gift comparable to what it gave her. The ocean replies, "You're tears of joy will now always be a part of me, you are now a part of our family. Your tears will add sparkle and light for the next traveler to see." The sea animals are dancing, celebrating. Fountains of sparkling water shoot out of the whale's blow holes. The sun is smiling and bathing her in a warm pink light."

*****

After the trip with Goldie, I only felt traces of fear about feeling space in my stomach and not consuming anything before bed. What was different was that I was strangely excited about being present and choosing my thoughts and feeling the feelings associated with good thoughts within the space. I was slowly able to relax into my body and peacefully accept the space. As Carl Jung states, "The greater the relaxation, the greater the inner acceptance of reality."

Instead of associating eating with helping me through my discomfort, I was practicing seeing compulsively eating as pushing the pause button in the discomfort. When I stopped eating, I was still in the same discomfort, just heavier. The food simply stopped me and weighed me down. Fear is heavy in my head. It becomes too heavy flows down to my chest and stops on my hips. I can either ask God to take it out of my head and change my beliefs, or I can eat or smoke and the fear transfers to extra weight on my body. So it doubles. I then have weight in my head and around my hips. Fear is heaviness, heaviness is fear. Heavy thoughts become heavy actions. Uncomfortable circumstances don't create a need to overeat; my thoughts about my circumstances create that need.

When I made the choice to accept the weak feelings with open arms, seeing the feelings as very small and me as very big, I could imagine picking up the crying feelings off the ground and holding them. In Identifying, Honoring, and Allowing the feelings in this way, they dissolved in the comfort of my embrace. I did the footwork, and I asked God to fill me from the top of my head to my toes with its spirit because I have to feel full with something. I needed to feel peace and power to my core. I asked God to show me how I could feel full, safe, grounded and loved. I knew that's really what I wanted

Can you believe that the next night God jumped out at me in Topanga Canyon? I was driving over Topanga from PCH talking to God about removing my fear of feeling alone and unloved before bed time. It so often spiraled into insomnia. As I asked God to help me, I rounded a corner and the fullest, brightest moon I'd ever seen shined so bright on me that I had to pull over. It had a reddish glow around it and I gasped as it took my breath. When I reached the top of Topanga, Moby's "Body Rock" was playing as all the lights of the valley flashed and danced to the beat. I felt like Goldie coming out of the darkness into a celebratory party!

Becoming Goldie was pivotal in my personal progress because it allowed me to take limitations off of myself. Feeling brave and protected in my superhero suit, I could allow God to show me miraculous demonstrations of his power beyond what I thought were possible. I imagined being love and feeling the comfort and peace in love. I saw that when Goldie focused her awareness on love pockets in her body, they light up in a pinkish red color. She smiles when she sees the light and speaks her intention to exude love from her body out into the Universe. She watches as the light radiates out from her body. A breeze picks it up and carries it to a man. It touches him and he feels warmth and comfort.

At this point, I still couldn't maintain a consistent connection to the love. It was as if I was floating in a pink cloud and out of nowhere I'd drop into an abyss. Just twelve hours after experiencing love exuding from inside my body, a tornado started to slowly spin in my chest. It sped up and was quickly out of control. I came off the ground like a helicopter. Outside circumstances started the engine and I added sugar. With each bite the helicopter flew higher until my world became just a small foggy speck on the map.

It seemed that the abyss was always waiting for me on Sundays. My mind would close up and I'd feel like I was trapped in a limited space where I couldn't see or feel the excitement of my life. It felt like getting thrown into first gear. It happened on Sundays and especially at night. Maybe it was the disappointment of not having a date with "the one" over the weekend or the dread of another week of mediocrity. I would try to think about all that I had to look forward to but it felt like it was far away, unreachable, separate from me. It looked like all the future possibilities were turning around and floating away and all I could do was watch them disappear. As I kept my eyes opened and my mouth closed, I realized it was the first Sunday night in months that I hadn't binged.

*****

I had discovered the spiritual disciplines that were setting me free from compulsive eating: forgiveness, surrender, losing judgment, planting the seeds of possibility, identifying negative beliefs and replacing them with positive beliefs. Becoming free was not a cognitive process. If that were the case, it would be easy. I would have just memorized the tools and regurgitated them from memory when I wanted to eat. That's one reason why diets didn't work for me. I knew in my brain what and how much to eat to be healthy and thin, but that never stopped me from bingeing. My process was a spiritual learning process, which meant having a new experience with sometimes the same circumstances in my life. I've heard people say that you will experience the same problem, for example, getting involved in dysfunctional relationships, until you learn the lesson and heal the dysfunctional pattern in yourself. I was talking with a friend about the way she found herself in the same relationship over and over, just with different men. I could relate.

What I learned is that I could be home alone on a Saturday or Sunday night and feel comfort and love. My circumstances hadn't changed, but I had changed. I slowly experienced a shift with the disciplines I had discovered. Similarly, my weight did not change until I began to have a new experience with my body. I didn't think I could love and accept my body being overweight. The biggest fallacy is that you can't love and accept your body before you lose the weight. A spiritual experience is an inside job. Some people change faster than others. So I practice the same spiritual disciplines because when I first started, they scratched the surface and with further practice, they began to penetrate to my center and heal me to my core.

*****

My hopes on the beach at Point Dume for my 30th birthday had come true to a certain extent. The last day of my 30th year I thought, "I am replacing irrational thinking with rational thinking. I'm not panicking and I'm not anxiety ridden. My stomach is half empty. It feels really good. I feel power. I see that opportunities are abundant and consistent. "

Well, the first week of being 31, I got an opportunity to practice the gift of rational thinking I had received for my 30th birthday. It was a Thursday morning. I woke up early to go to an 8:30 Bar Method exercise class in West LA. I knew it was a Level Two class and I was supposed to take at least five mixed classes before going, but I went anyway because I bought a one month unlimited pass for $100 and I hadn't been for five days. I got to class and the teacher asked if I'd been to five classes yet. When I said no, he said ok, but he was going to go fast and not stop to help me. I said ok and after a few minutes he came over and told me I needed to leave. Oh my God. I felt angry because I had woken up so early to go and angry at him for insulting me and being harsh about it. My pride was hurt because I didn't want the class to see that I wasn't good enough. My self esteem was hurt because I wanted to be someone who could handle the class. My ambition was hurt because I wanted to get a workout and be accepted. My security was threatened because I needed to be good enough and accepted to feel ok.

As I drove away, I took responsibility for going to the class knowing I was breaking the rules. I felt the feelings that I fear so much which were: feeling rejected, not good enough, looking bad, and disrespected. These feelings translated into, "if I was fifteen pounds lighter, I would have looked and been good enough to be accepted, therefore not alone". I felt these feelings intensely. My first reactive thought was to say no to these feelings and smoke. That felt justified for a minute. Then I reconsidered and heard the truth that to smoke would create more fear. Then I thought about eating. But then I paused and knew that wouldn't dissolve the feelings either. What I learned from the book, "Feel the Fear and Do It Anyway" enabled me to take responsibility and "know" that to avoid the feelings would create more fear and disturbance and a need to "fix". I was *really* proud of myself. I felt the fear and pain and took responsibility. I felt it and didn't avoid it by eating or smoking. That's probably why I got kicked out of the class. I didn't get a physical workout for my body but I jumped to the next level I've been climbing toward for years. I said to myself, "I handled it. I can handle it. I can do it. I'm not a victim. I am powerful and loving it. I am in control of my thoughts and actions. I am in control of fear."

My road to freedom was bumpy right up to the end. The awareness was glaring that whenever I did avoid discomfort, it physically manifested in my body, which could one day put me in the hospital with heart problems or lung cancer. It was undeniable. It was staring me in the face.

130

The fear created by avoiding fear was so much more painful than just feeling the discomfort and moving through it. In believing I had more power than the discomfort, I found the freedom inside the pain of bingeing and I kept moving forward. I identified more thoughts that were keeping me heavy:

1) thinking about 5pm (dinner) as the pleasure point of the day

2) thinking that dinner 5-6pm stabilizes me emotionally and mentally

3) associating feeling full with security and feeling half full with insecurity

I chose to change my focus by making 5-6pm my prime hour for service to other people. That gave me true fulfillment instead of making me feel painfully full.

*****

I had worked SO HARD and changed so much because I knew that if nothing changes, nothing changes. Deep and lasting change is often a longer process than one would wish. In the grand scheme of things, I see that a few years is a blip on the screen. Especially towards the end, it seemed like I might have taken a detour on my road to freedom from compulsive eating. With only a year to go on my road, I hit a dead end. It was midnight, August 30, 2005 when the four horsemen of terror, bewilderment, frustration, and despair visited for the last time:

"I've gained nine pounds in six days and I hate myself. I started praying, screaming on the way home from work because I continue to binge and continue to gain weight and continue to get more depressed. I don't believe I can stop bingeing and hating myself and gaining weight. I am afraid of myself. I am afraid that this person is going to continue to kill me. I want this person to die. I want to burn this evil person. I cannot be free with this person. This person has no will power and doesn't care about me. She says I'm different from thin people, that I'm not able to be disciplined, free, and happy. I hate her. She won't let me recover. Who is she and why won't she leave me the f##k alone? She says: "You can't recover; you will always overeat and be overweight no matter how hard you try. Your body is fat and embarrassing. You should be ashamed to go out and run and exercise. Your butt and legs are pitiful and disgusting. You are pathetic and weak and lazy and fat. You will never have a relationship because you can't stop eating. I am in control of you. You can go to self help meetings, you can read all the books you want, you can write, make phone calls, try to have a positive attitude, make gratitude lists, meditate, you can help others, but I will always – no matter what you do – make you binge and gain weight. You will never lose 20 pounds. You might lose a few and get a little more comfortable but you will never be free. You will always end up bingeing and alone. You will always live ashamed and alone with food because you are stuck – weak – unable to change. You will always be miserable. You won't be able to go to the beach in a bikini, or wear cute clothes, or eat like a normal person. You are fu##ed. Ha! No matter how hard you try, all this writing won't help – just when you get a little peace – BAM! You will just break – binge – and get fat. You will always be overweight because you are fu##ed!! Other people have sought help, become sane, and lost weight, but you can't.

Your lot in life is to be miserable and fat. You aren't strong enough to say no. You can sometimes say no but at some point you'll binge and want to die. You will never be free to be happy. Because I control you. You don't know anyone else. No one else is here. It's just us. You and me. Ha! I have control over you! You are screwed! FU##ED. You may as well be dead because every day is a struggle with food. You've lost all discipline and choice and strength. You have NO control because I control You!! God can't help you because I control You!! You won't live without me. I'm punishing you for being weak and stupid and unloved and unsuccessful. No one can help you. You are my robot. You – in the end – always fall into me. You believe me. I have you. You can't walk away.

I am ashamed of my body and ashamed for people to see me. I am ashamed of my relationship with food. I am ashamed of my weakness with food. I feel like I have no control over my eating. I can not say no to food or my thinking. I do not have the strength to change and say no. I do not deserve a thin body, free from obsession. I am angry that I'm fat. I'm angry that at some point I always binge, overeat and stay fat. I'm angry that I've let food have so much power over me. I'm angry at God for not removing the obsession. I hate being in my body. I hate my life. I can't change. I'm so angry at myself for eating every time I shouldn't. I'm angry that I don't eat like a normal person. I'm angry that I haven't been running or exercising. I hate that I don't want to get up in the morning. I hate myself and my body. I hate myself for not saying no. I hate this life of obsession and overeating.

I wish I could kill myself and start over with a new head and body. I want to die and start over with no anger, no judgment, no shame – with love, forgiveness, peace. I want to die.

I want to kill the person in me who says: "Just eat it, you are fat anyway, you won't lose any weight today anyway. Just eat it. It doesn't matter. You'll eat anyway. You are fat anyway. This won't hurt. You need to eat. You are empty. You can't run. You are too fat. Your butt is fat running down the street. Your thighs are fat. You are embarrassing. You are a disappointment. You will be crazy if you do lose weight and you are crazy now. You are stuck with food and fat. You won't fall in love because you are fat." I want to kill the person who eats when I don't want to eat. I want to kill the person who hates my body and eats. I want this person to fu##ing die - who feels less than skinny people. I want all the voices to die. The weak part that can't say no - or who says no but then eats anyway. The voice that says I can't be thin. Where am I?

I want a new person in my body. A new person who is strong, fierce, determined, disciplined, unafraid, confident in her ability to follow through, in control. I want a person to come into my body and take the place of this evil person who is trying to kill me. I want a new person who has a voice of strength, deserving, self-respect, and self- love. Who can keep the evil person far away. A new person who can beat the evil person to a pulp – who can literally beat the life out of the evil person. I want a new person to move into my body. I want her to tell me who she is – a stronger, disciplined - in complete control and totally self respecting person to move in and take over. And tell me that, yes, the old evil person

134

did control you but I have kicked it out and I am now inside you. You are mine now. I will show you how you will think and live. I am in control of your thoughts and actions. You are safe – with me now. The days of the evil one are over. I am in your body now."

In walking into the darkness of the dead end, I entered into a deeper power and freedom. I was so close. That night proved to be the darkest hour before the dawn. The last hour of the journey, however, would take a year. I was using the six disciplines more consistently. I was like the elephant that lived years of her life in shackles. When they are removed, the elephant often still walks in circles.

I had been in a prison cell for years. I now held the keys in my hand. As strange as it sounds, I was at times comfortable in my cell and afraid to go out into the bright shiny world. I wanted so desperately to walk out into it and be a part of it but the fear kept me inside. I decided I could walk out into freedom just a few steps at a time. When I would get scared and binge, I would pick up my tool of Forgiveness. I practiced surrendering to stomach hunger by giving myself IHA Moments. My tastes of freedom proved that anything was possible, so I continued to expand my positive beliefs. I kept getting up each time I fell. I could see a world of freedom right in front of me and I wasn't about to give up.

My fear of discomfort transformed into power when I shifted my perception. I saw that bingeing was like digging a hole and crawling into it to hide from the painful feelings. I saw the feelings as a dark swampy mass that groans deep guttural moans. It smells like sewage but always remains in the distance. When I sense the monster, I fear that it will slide,

135

as if on a flat escalator, to me and cover me up. It was the same fear that I had in childhood nightmares when I was afraid that if the monster heard me or saw me move, it would "get me" so I would stay frozen under the covers. What I noticed as an adult was that the mass is stuck, I'm not. However, because of my past experience of being stuck as a teenager at my parents' house, I believed that all I could do was hide. I remembered that I could see the monster in the distance and choose to keep moving. I became less afraid of the "monster" when I chose to see it as just a harmless mass of energy. That empowered me to keep getting up, stronger and lighter on my journey forward, instead of down.

My IHA moments in December of 2005 echo what I believe many men and women so deeply crave. These moments also raised my comfort level on the hunger/ full scale. I deeply craved the affection that comes from loving physical contact with a man. I needed to be embraced. Monthly massages didn't satiate my deprived body. I wanted a man whom I loved to hold me, rub my back and tell me he loves me. I felt like I could not or would not get enough of the love, connection and affection that I needed. I felt helpless over my feelings of loneliness. A blanket of sadness covered my body. It hurt to feel needy and not get the need for love and physical affection satisfied. Unmet needs were still intolerable at times. Part of me still felt like the only way to stop the longing was to fill myself with food. Every bite dulled the acute loneliness but left me feeling more unlovable. It took a long time for me to admit the truth - that I craved true love and affection. When I allowed myself to feel vulnerable, I asked myself how I could tolerate these feelings without food. I decided that I *could* stay open by not filling myself with food. I wanted to be open to the real love and comfort that I truly wanted. I was willing to feel vulnerable.

The following week I experienced a serious shift in my ability to tolerate my feelings without eating. Instead of going to bed at a six or seven, I went to bed at a four on the hunger/full scale. The truth about vulnerability was that it allowed love to touch me on a deeper lever. I could pause in the moment and make a choice to wait for hunger. For the first time, I craved hunger. Now I know it was also a craving for truth. I felt like Wonder Woman with this newfound power of choice. When hungry, I ate to a six or seven and felt satisfied instead of stuffed. I loved walking away from a meal feeling light and playful.

*****

2006 marked the last year in my eating disorder and the first year in freedom. My therapist Mina, a guy named Gary, and Goldie helped me to activate my unlimited supply of divine power and comfort I'd always craved.

The most powerful tool I received from Mina was the magnifying glass. She explained that lasting life change usually isn't a result of a one-time quick decision. She encouraged me to make "small" changes. When you look at a big structure under a magnifying glass, you see that it's made up of many small pieces. Putting a "pause" between the impulsive need to eat and the actual first bite was a small change that would create space for a big shift. This is what happened:

"I haven't written for a while and I just want to unload stuff that's in me, update and get clear. So, my thinking and actions are changing drastically since I've been seeing Mina again. She's a Godsend. It started last weekend. Friday was a day of small resistances to eating outside of stomach hunger until I finally caved and ate donuts on Melrose. But – I had **a lot** of discipline and resistance before that. Saturday I worked. I had resisted a binge a lot of times then the pressure got to the breaking point. I was about to eat a box of laxatives then start bingeing – but I paused in the moment and called Mina and left a message. I ended up eating junk and decided I was going to call my friend Catia, who I had plans with, lie and tell her I couldn't get off work early to go out with her. We had planned for a month to go to the Dragonfly in Hollywood to hear her boyfriend's band, "Orson" play. The phone rang. I had a feeling it was Mina and didn't really want to talk to her because that would interrupt my binge, but I answered the phone. I told her I was going to keep eating and –miraculously- by the time I hung up with her I decided I actually could stop eating – go to the show – and not eat anymore! MIRACLE. I actually did that! Sunday I still felt heavy and jammed up but I went to Runyon for a hike. I was sitting in the car and decided to drive back home – but after ten minutes of sitting – I got out of the car and did my hike/run. That was contrary action. I ended up bingeing and throwing up a few days later and felt sick and tired the next day. I didn't want to run, struggled a lot over that but let myself off the hook. I ate two cookies from my favorite bakery, "Mani's", – *but changed my thinking and behavior and didn't continue to eat sh#t"*.

I got incredible insight while talking with Mina about how I panic on Sundays and usually binge. She kept it simple by instructing me to "listen and accept, approve of, validate and support that sixteen year old – who had *really* shitty Sundays." She said that having a conversation with that scared, impulsive sixteen year old would reduce my anxiety. Although I became stuck in a binge cycle while unable to express myself, I now, as an adult, could allow her to express everything that was bottled inside. My inability to communicate and be heard at sixteen was crippling but I was "learning to walk again". As the Foo Fighters sing, "I believe I've waited long enough, where do I begin yeeaahhh!" I needed to yell like Dave Grohl – and be heard by a stadium of fans cheering me on. I became a captive audience to my teenager. I let her rage. Inside her I found the heartbroken four year old whose Daddy left for the first time. I listened to her cry. I held her without trying to change her feelings. Susan Stiffelman explains so brilliantly in her book, *Parenting Without Power Struggles,* that the best way to support your children through their pain is to allow them the time and space to feel it before you offer them a solution.

I carried so much energy inside that it felt scary at times to let it out. I told Mina that I felt out of control when my body was thin and sexy, as if I was afraid of being unrestrained and "too much". It was as if the extra weight kept my energy safely anchored. She said that the control, restraint and discipline that I am now using with food will permeate all areas of my life. I would actually be stronger and more in control of my decisions, actions and life in a thinner body. I *could* trust myself. She was right again.

Like clockwork, the right book at the right time jumped off the shelf to teach me just how to hone and channel the wild spirit that held my creative energy. Two paragraphs into Dan Millman's book, *The Life You Were Born to Live,* and I was so blown away I had to take a breather outside. My birth number, according to the Life Purpose System (from the Pythagorean Heritage) means double creativity and abundance. Millman explained that with as much energy that's inside me, I must release it somehow because it cannot be contained. It *will* be expressed either negatively or positively. If I don't release it positively through vigorous exercise and creativity, then I will use an addiction like food, nicotine, alcohol or drugs to suppress it. I was convinced that February day in 2006 that the positive purpose of my anxiety was creative writing. The anxiety would start to creep up on me and become a monkey crawling up my back with me unable to get it off. It came to visit daily. I couldn't tolerate how it felt and I couldn't make it leave. Oftentimes only a binge would relieve the anxiety, but I found that when I wrote from a creative perspective, it lifts. It was clear that I could either write or eat. I chose to write with the faith that the anxiety would lift. It worked.

One morning, my e-mail from the "Daily Guru" reminded me of my favorite Einstein quote, "Imagination is more important than knowledge. Knowledge is limited, imagination encircles the world." Getting to know Goldie was proof that imagination can be used as a doorway to reality. Like Goldie, I was waking up on the shore of a new world. I needed all the power she gave me to move through the last leg of the tour.

I felt resistance at the beginning of a run one morning. My energy was low and I just didn't feel energized or optimistic about the day. I became Goldie and saw a calm, blue ocean filling my head. Then a big yellow-orange liquid ball of sun set from the crown of my head and sunk down through my body and out my feet into the Earth. The warm light permeated every cell of my body and I contentedly thanked God for another spiritual experience.

Staying on track using the tools I had discovered was becoming easier. I was trusting my God and my body more and needed food less. As I looked forward into my future at what I could give, the fear of the past repeating itself continued to diminish. I had stopped attaching pleasure thoughts to food and had changed my belief to the reality that when I allow space in my stomach, possibility emerges. It took a lot of practice to rewire my brain. I mistakenly associated comfort with eating for so many years that attaching the reality of pain with overeating took more time than I hoped. Susan Stiffelman uses the image of "thoughts as drugs" to illustrate the effect one's belief can have on one's action. She explains in *Parenting Without Power Struggles*, "Now, as with any pill or drug, when you swallow it, you're under the influence of the drug that it contains, which in this case is the influence of that belief. The story you've chosen to believe infiltrates your consciousness, and now you're at the mercy of its effect on you." I was wide awake to the truth about food and love. The less I used food in an attempt to feel comfort, the more my heart opened.

Nothing brought out fear and vulnerability like falling in love. After jumping off the roller coaster of notoriously unavailable men, I met Gary.

He had the look that I was always attracted to, dark hair, green eyes, and a big build, but his energy was different from other guys I had gone out with. Those guys would bust into a room like a bull, spewing sexual energy all over the place. Gary was more reserved. He was full of sexy, attractive energy, but he revealed it slowly. I was intrigued by his slightly mysterious nature. He was a veterinarian and I respected the intelligence and perseverance it took for him to become successful. He was not an actor or a musician and he was from Santa Monica. That was refreshing. He had traveled all over the world surfing and exploring different cultures. At a party at a mutual friend's home one night, he told a story about riding his motorcycle to the Motley Crue concert downtown. What? He didn't seem the type. He then took his shirt off to jump in the pool and that's when the dragon over his shoulder caught my eye. When he told me got the tattoo in Thailand from a local who used the traditional bamboo stick with the needle on the end, I was hooked. He was tough too. Tattoos, motorcycles, and Motley Crue. He surprised me. My first read on him was off. I thought he was a nice, quiet young man who played it safe. Who was this guy? I wanted to find out.

We went out to lunch the next week and I'll never forget the way I felt cradled by his strapping shoulders when he hugged me. He enveloped me with his strength. His muscles weren't all pumped up like gym rats, he was just big and I loved the way his body felt hugging mine. I remember the first few months we dated, we would hug each other so tight for so long that our arms would be sore the next day. Seriously!

This relationship was different for me because I didn't feel like I was on a mad roller coaster ride. He called every day and didn't play games. His consistent presence touched a place in me where access had always been denied. I had prayed for an open mind and a new experience with men. My fear of intimacy had decreased and my curiosity about commitment had increased. Fear would prove to keep me alone, in weak moments, in the midst of falling in love.

My relationship with Gary allowed me to open my heart slowly. Fear slammed it shut again quite often at first. If I didn't stay connected to the God inside me, then I couldn't stay connected to Gary. My vulnerability felt safer when I remembered what I learned through my experience with Matt and my therapist, Darcy. I remembered that I have a lifetime supply of love and comfort that is waiting for me at all times. God put it inside at birth and it's indestructible. I could access it at any time if I'm willing to shift my perception and open my mind. Running and meditating on this bliss inside activated a spiritual experience beyond what any man could give me, or take away. Eating less and remaining open became easier. Using "God given love and comfort is alive inside me" as a mantra made me want to feel it, instead of numbing myself with food. I allowed myself to get hungry before we went out to eat. I wanted to enjoy our meals out because if I wasn't hungry, eating didn't feel good.

With an open heart, I experienced a deluge of heavy emotion. The tidal wave started when I stopped by Gary's office on my way home form work one night. When he hugged me against the wall in the parking lot, I felt like I was embracing and being embraced with pure, gentle, raw energy. I was afraid to let go. My chest tightened. I held him as close as I could. His arms were wrapped completely around me as my head rested on his shoulder. I tried to choke down my feelings of vulnerability. I was afraid to be separated from him. His presence felt like an exquisitely precious, valuable gift that was not yet mine. As we held each other, I broke the silence to tell him that I realized how important he is in my life and how sad I was that I didn't get to spend the previous night with him. My heart felt bruised. I became acutely aware of the love I felt for this man. I clung to his arm like an infant fearing the inevitable separation and the slight possibility that I could never see him again. Tears fell from my eyes.

I cried like a baby from the moment I drove out of his parking lot in Santa Monica to the moment I drove into mine in West Hollywood. I listened to Paul McCartney sing "Maybe I'm Amazed" with personal experience for the first time.

That raw vulnerability I was so afraid of felt surprisingly good in a way that was new and awkward. I was more open than I'd ever been. This is what it felt like to be alive. Feeling feelings in their raw form without numbing them with food was like gasping a breath of fresh air. I wanted to live before I died and I was once again experiencing the truth that feelings won't kill you but avoiding them will.

Anger was one of those feelings I had a tendency to avoid since I was a little girl. Denying it, for the most part, for 30 years had turned a normal human emotion into a landfill of toxicity. Anger was dark, heavy energy inside me that I was tired of carrying. I continued to admit that I was angry that I couldn't eat massive amounts and be skinny and that I had to just feel the feelings instead of eat. Speaking my anger or writing it on paper relieved the pressure that was boiling inside. I felt lighter every time I acknowledged anger and expressed it in a healthy way without judgment. It became easier and more natural to wait for hunger and stop eating before I felt too full.

Identifying, honoring, and allowing my feelings, in the moment, were dissolving my desire to eat. Telling the truth when I was angry was empowering! Expressing anger in a healthy way helped me become light and free.

The summer of 2006 marked my ability to *consistently* experience bingeing triggers without eating. The small isolated changes were becoming my new way of life. Feeling sick and going to sleep were monsters that I had now befriended. They no longer devoured my dreams. Fear was shrinking and my power was dominating my life!

I was feeling so much more comfortable in my skin that I decided to try to meditate sitting still. The circus had stopped and set up shop in my head once again but I was willing to try. I closed my eyes and opened my mind. The curtains parted in the middle of my forehead and opened wide.

All the different voices and thoughts became characters in my head, sliding down a red carpet out of my forehead! Weee! Each one was like a mini person and they were all saying the thoughts in my brain. It was loud....but funny, like a party! They tumbled out and down but a few voices were left whispering inside. The janitor swept them out and down

145

the slide, and then dimmed the lights. I was left with a clean, clear, peaceful, quiet head! Ahhh.

After my meditation I hiked up Runyon Canyon listening to Peter Gabriel's "Shaking the Tree". On the way up I felt like I was in a video game shooting out bullets of love, magic and comfort from my chest. I hit a few hikers who looked way too serious with snowballs of humor. Splat! – right in the face. I took a deep breath and blew out stars of inspiration and hope into the eyes of despair. And I couldn't help shooting a few guys with an aphrodisiac, just for fun. The object of my game was to hit as many people as possible. The most points were scored when I hit the most troubled person. If I hit someone with a star of hope who was contemplating suicide, all the bells and whistles would sound, the lights would flash and the game would show his life up to that moment. Then it would show him becoming armed with love to hit other people and he would become the player.

Living in this 4-D world sure beat living in a head full of fear. I decided to try the sitting still meditation again. I closed my eyes, opened my mind and Goldie appeared. She jumped into my body and showed me how to activate divine power on a daily basis. As I looked inside my body I saw flickers of light sparkling all over. Circular love magnets in my hands, feet and chest were drawing in all kinds of positive energy. The light from under my skin radiated outside of my body. The "railroad tracks" of veins and arteries connected the magnets of divine essence to my brain. Train cars loaded with sparkles traveled to my brain, infusing my thoughts with creativity and inspiration. My brain was a glowing love factory! Like the

North Pole at Christmas! I accidentally discovered more power when I bent over to stand up. As my back stretched, light escaped from between my ribs and vertebrae. I felt like a super hero!

*****

On August 2, 2006 I said the prayer of St. Francis of Assissi. I was on the Stairmaster listening to Guns N' Roses thinking about helping a friend who was struggling with sobriety. She was tormented by a head full of fear, as I once was, and I wanted to remind her that she could turn her thoughts and actions over to the care of loving, comforting and fun God. I made a mental note to tell her that she's safe in sobriety now – does she want to get lost in the darkness again? I wanted her to imagine basking in the sunlight of the spirit. Then the realization washed over and through me with power and light that I too was in a colorful, sparkly, new world. I had walked out of the desert and into freedom. It struck me that I was standing at the gates of paradise looking around wide- eyed, like a child entering Disneyland for the first time. I realized that Guns N' Roses "Knockin' on Heaven's Door" had begun to play as I had the awakening. I started sobbing, overwhelmed with the presence of God. Power and inspiration had filled my body to overflow. I was free.

*****

Maintaining freedom was, and still is a daily practice. As I go about my day, I am faced with two paths. I look at the narrow, dark path of mediocrity and hear a voice say "You're not ready for the brilliant path. It's unknown and scary. You know this one, just take it." It takes me to the same boring places everyday. I look at the bright path of positivity and I hear, "Nothing can hurt you here. You are armed with love and light. If this path isn't better than mediocrity, you are free to return to it. You can do this. You know where to go, people are waiting to show you around and your work here is way more gratifying!"

The six disciplines I uncovered on my fifteen year journey keep me free today. I discovered that my body was the package that carried a piece of God, given to me on my Birth Day. I had removed the ribbon, thrown out the stuffing of negativity, dug to the bottom and found my Bellyful of Bliss that had been sparkling my whole life.

PART 2

THE HOW:

Disciplines for Freedom

The six disciplines are the tools I used that set me free from compulsive eating. These spiritual principles don't always free me from the pain and discomfort that is simply a part of life. They are in no way a one way ticket to happiness. That's never been my goal. The disciplines simply relieve me of the mental obsession with food and my body, and they relieve me from the desire to compulsively eat. This is an uncovering process of what's blocking your Bellyful of Bliss. You will be removing layers of anger, excess food, judgment, and limited beliefs to clear the channel to your inner power. Feeling just one minute of bliss each day is enough for me to be satisfied. I remember promising God that if He would free me from my eating disorder, I would do ANYTHING to help other people become free from theirs. I am humbled and honored that I can hold up my end of the bargain and inspire freedom to you.

Chapter 4

Forgiveness Dissolves Fat

"Forgiveness is the fragrance that the violet sheds on the heel that has

crushed it."   - Mark Twain

If you are a compulsive eater, you have experienced enough self loathing to last a lifetime. My self hate grew with each compulsive bite. Every time I looked in the mirror, every time I tried on jeans and they were too tight, every time I compared myself to skinny girls, I hated myself more. I was so angry with myself for overeating after every firm resolve to stop. It's crystal clear in retrospect that the anger did not control my eating or help me lose weight. I read books by Louise Hay, Judi Hollis and Sondra Ray that convinced me to flirt with forgiveness. I was so afraid that if I forgave myself for bingeing, then I would continue to binge, as if forgiveness was permission to continue harmful behavior. I confused forgiveness and self- acceptance with staying stuck. I was afraid that forgiving myself meant that I was just making peace with overeating and being overweight. I learned that forgiveness addresses past behavior, and was the invitation to stop hurtful behavior in the future.

For many years, forgiveness made me feel vulnerable, as if anger was emotional protection. The anger at others, and especially at myself, was like a brick wall I built around my heart, keeping me alone. When I began to forgive myself, the wall started to crumble. I began to feel warmth from the light shining through and it felt comforting and safe. The truth about forgiveness is that it enables the healing that melts away fat. If I could have stopped compulsively overeating years ago I would have. I tried every method with all the strength I could muster and bingeing was just inevitable at times. Forgiveness puts the brakes on the runaway train of compulsive eating. Forgiveness is power. Forgiveness is the salve that soothes your self inflicted wounds. When you practice forgiveness, you begin to release the weight of the past from your body.

It's just as important to forgive the people you feel have hurt you the most. Think back to when you first started compulsively eating. Who let you down, or didn't provide what you needed. Who broke your heart, abandoned you, or abused you? No matter what they did, you have the choice today to forgive him/her so that you can be free. Forgiveness doesn't mean that what they did is acceptable, it simply means that you're letting go of the pain that's blocking your power.

The HOW:

If it feels dishonest to forgive the person you see in the mirror today, then visualize the "you" when you began to use food to soothe your soul.

1. How old were you when you first began compulsively eating?

2. What was happening at home, in your family? What were your underlying thoughts and feelings at that time? That "little you" is still hurting and needs comfort. Find a picture of yourself at the age when you began compulsively eating and you can begin to forgive and feel compassion for her.

3. If you feel resistance in forgiving others, consider how he/she was raised and what kind of pain they might have suffered. Understanding where another person is coming from can explain why their harmful behavior might make sense. One can't hurt another unless he/she is also hurting. Imagine the person you resent as a child, who is hurting. Feeling compassion for him/her enables forgiveness to flow. You're not excusing their behavior or letting them off the hook, you're trying to understanding them so that you can forgive and be free.

4. Make a list:

What thoughts, feelings and actions haven't you forgiven yourself for?

What are your regrets?

What are you angry at yourself about?

Write EVERYTHING that comes to mind.

5. Begin your forgiveness practice:

Turn every sentence from your list of anger and regret into a sentence of forgiveness:

"I forgive you, (your name) for (thoughts, feelings, actions)".

(My lists of anger, regret, and forgiveness affirmations filled an entire notebook.)

6. Mirror Forgiveness:

I learned this exercise from Louise Hay's book "You Can Heal Your Life". When I first tried to look at myself in the mirror and say "I forgive you, Amy. I love you, I really love you," I couldn't do it. I could not look into my own eyes without feeling a sense of repulsive shame. The anger I felt towards myself was so strong that before I could look into my eyes and speak from a place of forgiveness, I had to write all of my forgiveness affirmations on paper. Then I was able to look into my eyes without feeling disgust. I now can look into my eyes, speak forgiveness and love, and it actually feels true today.

"I forgive you, (your name) for (thoughts, feelings, actions), you were hurting."

"I love you, (your name) I really love you."

Chapter 5

Sweet Surrender:

Trusting the Brilliance in Your Belly

"Surrender, or go crazy."   -Anonymous

When I found out I was pregnant I knew I was entering unchartered territory. My old ways of trying to manage my weight through restriction or purging would not work during pregnancy. Weighing my self daily as a means of attempted control would only reveal the truth of a healthy pregnancy – weight gain! I was in a serious dilemma. I felt cornered with no way to attempt to control my weight in this new, nine month state of being. Clearly I was going to gain weight and obviously I would need to satisfy certain food cravings. I also knew that if I treated feeling tired, sick and emotional with food like I normally did, I would eat like crazy and blow up before I even started showing.

Convinced of my past inability to control my eating, I had a moment of clarity, which I knew to my core was the truth. It was a strong intuitive thought that was as clear to me as my inability to manage my eating disorder. It was simpler than any diet, therapy or exercise. The truth that was revealed was to *eat when my stomach was hungry and to stop before I felt too full. Just take this pregnancy one hunger and one feeding at a time.* That made perfect sense to me. If I eat a moderate amount when my stomach is hungry then there probably won't be much left over to turn into unhealthy fat. I experienced tastes of freedom from this simple idea in the past, but I never had the ability to *consistently* wait for stomach hunger or stop eating before I was too full. But being pregnant, I felt a stronger motivation to listen to my body and treat it with respect. It wasn't just my body; it was a precious baby I was caring for as well.

This motivation, however, was also powered by my long standing foe: fear, which now began to act as a friend. For the first time, fear acted as a positive motivator instead of a negative force. The fear of feeling despair without psychiatric medication that followed a binge, along with raging pregnancy hormones, was terrifying. I was afraid of the out of control spiral into darkness. That was the main fear that motivated a shift into the freedom of surrender.

I was also afraid of pumping massive amounts of junk into my precious little fetus. I knew that on some level he could feel what I felt and would be affected by the binge. I saw an image of a hose pumping an overload of junk into my baby. I saw ice cream, cookies, bread, chips - all my binge food - crammed into him and his little body trying to digest the junk. The fear of needing to vomit after a binge, even though I wouldn't want to, was also a positive motivator. Vomiting always felt violent and slightly traumatic, more to my spirit than to my body, but I vomited at times, despite the pain. The image of my baby being shaken up or physically stressed due to vomiting broke my heart and also helped motivate a series of surrenders which set me free from compulsive eating.

The third motivating fear was of gaining more weight than my body needed for nourishment. I imagined being fat after my baby was born, feeling depressed, and the dread of trying to lose the weight. I knew I would breast feed, so getting back on medication was not an option for me. I decided I could gain as little weight as was possible so that I would feel healthy and happy after he was born. I was aware that I was at a higher risk for postpartum depression because I lived with severe mood swings pre-pregnancy. I knew that being fat postpartum would be more than I could handle along with the lack of sleep that comes with a newborn. Being tired was always a huge trigger for me to overeat. Facing unhealthy weight gain and lack of sleep was enough to deal with. I was afraid that extra fat on top of that would put me over the edge mentally and emotionally.

I was also motivated by a desire to be a hot mamma! I wanted to be thin and healthy like other new moms I had seen. I didn't want fat to be a damper on the happiest time in my life. So considering nine months of being sick, tired and emotional more often was overwhelming. The only way to deal with my feelings without medication and without food was to take this new state of body and mind one day at a time, one hunger at a time. This simple concept is what I surrendered to, which helps keep me free to this day, seven years later. Surrendering became the key to unlock the prison door that had kept me in solitary confinement. For the first time in fifteen years I began to *live* in a world of freedom and peace.

For me, the ability to surrender depends on what I'm surrendering to. I had surrendered many things in my life already with a positive result including alcohol, drugs, cigarettes and unhealthy relationships, but food was my survival mechanism for what felt like life threatening feelings. If I don't trust what I'm surrendering to, I'll continue to rely on a weaker method even if it isn't working. Therein lay the need for proof instead of blind faith. I remember a friend telling me that it was fine to have big dreams but I needed more that just blind faith, to which I immediately responded, "Oh I have faith, but it's anything but blind!" Hindsight is 20/20. I read a passage from a spiritual recovery book when I was twenty years old that I prayed to be true in my life which stated, "When we look back we realize that the things which came to us when we put ourselves in God's hands were better than anything we could have planned." I began to make a list of instances in my life where God had already given me experiences better than I planned. This list formed the foundation upon which my faith grew.

My concept of God has grown and changed over the years. My first beliefs about God were formed in the Methodist church as a child. I always believed that God is forgiving and loving but I realized upon further investigation that my concept of God was limited, boring and small. My concept of God grew as a result of what I learned from other religions and finally expanded to an energy field that I could see in nature. I began to believe that it was possible for me to feel, see, and hear God in a more powerful and creative way, beyond what I had ever experienced. I had read many spiritual books and believed that if it was possible for the various writers to have miraculous demonstrations of God in their life, then it was possible for me too. My finite mind can't understand an infinite God, but I knew that in order for me to surrender completely, it would help to be able to at least describe the Power to whom I was surrendering. I took my dictionary off the shelf and looked up the definitions of words that I believe describe God, like unlimited power, creativity, abundance and love. Being an educated woman, I knew what the words meant, but I was open to having a new experience and expanding my knowledge. I have had many experiences that were humanly inexplicable. I believed that a higher power gave me intuition, the right person showed up at the right time or I had the power to do something I'd never been able to do before. I wrote about the "God Shots" in my life and in others' where they saw, felt or heard God. By the time I finished writing, my concept was personal to me and I was actually excited to surrender to it!

I began to see expressions of God more often and more clearly in other people and in nature. As a result, I began to feel the peace, love and excitement of God in my daily life. When I prayed and received an intuitive answer I felt security. When I ran and felt empowered, I knew it was God's energy flowing through me. I'll never forget the creative electricity that shot through me at the David Bowie concert. It was a warm night under the stars at the Greek Theater in Hollywood.

Experiencing the combination of nature's beauty, soul shaking rock and roll and the energy of thousands of David Bowie fans singing the same song together brought to tears to my eyes. I felt like I was experiencing God's creativity on a higher level. Now, I can remember the euphoric feeling in my body at that concert as a way to re-feel God's power. Any time I get goose bumps or feel a sense of awe and wonder, I know its God's energy activated in my body. Whenever I want to eat when I'm not hungry or eat past full, I remember that I can eat and bury my bliss, or I can surrender to feeling God and be naturally thin and healthy.

I consider my body a divine creation. It knows how to work perfectly without much help from my mind. Each organ does its job to run my body whether I know what it's doing or not. That includes my stomach. When it needs food I feel space or hear grumbly sounds. If I pay attention to how my stomach feels while I'm eating instead of what my mind wants, I'll get the satisfied signal and stop eating. If I ignore it and keep eating, it stretches and I feel uncomfortable.

I noticed that my stomach needed only half of the portions I was used to eating. I have to admit, that was disappointing at first because I still love to eat. Now I *like* to eat small portions a few times a day and a bigger meal once a day. I have also noticed that my body feels more energized when I eat mostly fruit, vegetables, and healthy protein. As long as I feed my body plenty of pure, power food, I can eat my favorite dessert and still feel light and strong.

My pregnancy made it easier for me to reconnect with the bliss inside. Surrendering to the power that was growing my baby was humbling.

Letting go of mental control over eating and managing my weight to the perfect intelligence that breathes my body and pumps my heart made sense. My body stays alive with little help from my mind, so why not let my brilliant body signal when it needs food? It does a great job of running the rest of the machine! When I think of it like that it seems arrogant of me to let my mind decide when and how much to eat.

Surrendering to the hunger/full signal is also a sign of respect. I see my body as God's creation in that it was not formed by a human mind. I was often in a state of awe during my pregnancy. The presence of a power greater than my mind living inside my body became undeniable. I don't have the power or intelligence to run my body. Some magnificent force, a more intelligent energy inside my body is running hundreds of functions, even when I'm asleep. I never have to say to my eye, "Ok, see the green in that tree. Nose, smell that freshly cut grass." It just works and I have very little information on what's happening backstage. I didn't hook up his umbilical cord to my placenta and tell my baby to eat! I didn't wake up in week twelve, look at my to-do list and start making his fingernails. The Creative Intelligence grew my baby and my body and I knew I could trust surrendering to this power. I felt safe letting go of my ideas about what to eat when and letting God take over. I felt convinced that this journey into healthy weight gain was the beginning of a relationship built on trust and respect between my mind and body.

This process of surrender also brought about an almost exciting curiosity. With the surrender to eat when my body signaled hunger, I also surrendered what I would eat. I knew that during pregnancy your body often craves what it needs to grow the baby, and I wanted to give my baby what he needed. I began to feel what my body wanted to eat instead of my mind. I remember craving oranges late at night-not orange juice but oranges. I also craved broccoli salad. Look, my mind has NEVER craved oranges or broccoli. Clearly, my body needed vitamin C and calcium. The best part of eating what my body asked for was the feeling of satisfaction and completeness my body gave back to me. It was a feeling of balance that no thoughts could give me. I began to crave that feeling of balanced satisfaction after I ate what my body asked for when it was hungry. It was a grounded desire instead of a mind obsessed urgency to stuff my body, mute my thoughts and numb my feelings. This state of surrender and respect to my body felt really good. Letting my body take over created a lot of quiet space in my mind.

For the first time I realized that waiting for hunger did not mean waiting for emptiness. The idea of becoming empty was scary to me, as if I might disappear or float away. It's no wonder I kept my stomach full to avoid feeling a void. Empty is the last thing I want to feel! To me, empty means hollow, alone, vulnerable and weak. When I hear "empty", I think of a vacant, lifeless house. I guess there's nothing really wrong with an empty house but it's nowhere I'd like to live. I want to live in a home full of things I love, like vibrant colors, sounds of laughter and love, beautiful images, comfort and peace. Similarly, my body is a home to my spirit; therefore it's naturally full of God's energy. When my body is clean and clear I can easily hear God speaking to me as the still, small voice in my gut. I actually look forward to feeling space in my stomach and hearing the occasional audible growl! I've discovered that vulnerability + fear =

food, but vulnerability + faith = freedom. Today I touch the sweet spot in my belly where God lives each time I surrender to vulnerability.

I realized that the more attention I focused on sensations in my stomach, the less I thought about stuffing it. I never knew that body awareness could quiet the chatter in my head. My way of turning down the noise in my head, or trying to feel connected to something, was to eat! I began practicing body consciousness by paying attention to the feeling of stomach hunger and fullness. When I was pregnant it was easy to feel awe and wonder for the little ball of love in my belly. After he left my body and came into this world I realized that *I* am that ball of magical, miraculous love energy that was once inside my mother's belly! Surrendering to stomach hunger and trusting the brilliance in my belly was the beginning of my love affair with my body.

Years before I became free, I experienced moments of the peace that comes with surrender. I didn't yet know for sure that surrendering to stomach hunger was *the* answer but I knew that I was baffled by the insanity of bingeing and purging or restricting. I remember praying on my hands and knees in the bathroom after a particularly painful binge, begging God to help me. It was a "Help me God, I'll do anything!" prayer followed by a "knowing" to just let go of the fight. The next words I heard myself say to God were, "I don't even know how to surrender. Please show me." The peace inside that followed was profound. It was like the calm after the storm. The tornado had touched down again and left my body and mind destroyed but I felt relief in the stillness.

I've heard some people say that surrender is not a conscious choice but that one must "be surrendered". I'm not sure about that. I know that praying for willingness to surrender and to be shown how worked for me. One of the most effective prayers I used was, "God, please set aside everything I think I know about you, me, and my eating disorder, for an open mind and a new experience. Help me to see the truth." Knowing that, in surrender, I didn't have to let go of, or refute everything I knew but instead, I simply had to set it aside and try something new. That was doable. If you are still struggling to manage and control your eating, I invite you to step out of the ring, wave your white flag, and surrender to stomach hunger.

So HOW exactly do you surrender? Remember that surrender relieves the mental obsession about when to eat, what to eat and how much to eat. You are surrendering to power. You are surrendering to the perfect, innate, God given signal in your belly.

HOW to lose weight or maintain a healthy weight:

Here are some practical tips to help you wait to eat until you feel hunger at a "2" and stop eating at a "6" on the hunger scale:

1. Your goal is to touch the "2" and "6" 3 times a day. To do this, cut your portions in half. Remember, your body doesn't need food unless it's hungry.

2. If you want to feel more alive, eat more alive foods! I usually eat fruit for breakfast, veggies and protein for lunch, and more veggies, protein, and some sort of yummy carbohydrate for dinner. My heaviest meal is

166

usually dinner. Lighter food = a lighter body, and higher energy food (fruit and vegetables) = higher energy body. I still eat pizza, cheeseburgers, and French fries on occasion. I eat what my body wants and it usually wants healthy food.

3. Just for fun, try to guess what time you'll feel the "2". At first you'll probably be surprised at how long it takes your body to burn off excess food (energy) in order to get hungry again. You'll also probably be disappointed, at first, in how little your stomach needs to feel satisfied at a "6". Pretty soon though, living between a "2" and "6" will feel so great that you won't even want to let yourself get too hungry (a "0" or "1") or too full (a "7-10" on the hunger scale).

4. When you're waiting for the "2" but you want to eat, ask yourself, "What if I didn't eat right now? What if I waited to feel a healthy "2" hunger? How would that feel?" And more importantly, "What can I do until I get hungry? What can I do that I love, or that is productive? What am I really craving?" You are learning to live a life that you love in between your meals.

5. So you've eaten to a "6" on the hunger scale but you want to finish what's on your plate. Your stomach is satisfied. Your body doesn't need any more food. Pause. Ask yourself, "What if I put my plate away right now? What would happen if this was the end of my meal? How would it feel to leave this meal feeling light?" Do you need emotional or physical comfort? It's not on your plate. Excessive food has kicked your ass. It's time to start taking care of yourself. What's the next nourishing action you need to take to nurture your fun, productive, sexy life? Remember, as

soon as you get hungry again, you can eat! The food's not going anywhere!

6. Imagine how great you will feel waking up the next morning feeling clear, without having overeaten the day before.

HOW to feel full of God so that you don't stuff yourself full of food:

1. Shift your awareness from the thoughts in your head to the sensations in your belly. What do you feel? What do you see?

2. A belief in God is not necessary to surrender to stomach hunger, although it gave me a sense of comfort that I craved. If you'd like to expand your concept of God, consider the following questions:

What is your concept of God?

Can you supersize your concept, or make it juicer? Do you believe God is the source of love? creativity? fun? passion? freedom? abundance? peace? excitement? hope? What words do you use to describe God? Have you put limits on God?

Is there a time in your life when you felt the presence of God (good), or knew that God must have been involved in something good that happened?

The more you focus on God (love), knowing that it is inside of you and outside of you, the less you will want to eat outside of stomach hunger.

Chapter 6

IHA Moments:

Lose Judgment and Lose Weight

"The primary cause of unhappiness is never the situation but your thoughts about it."

― Eckhart Tolle

Identify, Honor, and Allow your feelings in this present moment.

Judgment has strangled your spirit and trapped you in the darkness. When you are in serious pain, suffering with an eating disorder, burying your bliss with each compulsive bite, you are burying the life force inside. Imagine laying on a gurney. You've been stabbing yourself in the heart with self hate. Your body is bloody. You are suffering on that gurney. You are on life support. Don't waste time by judging yourself, the way you look, or how you shouldn't be on the gurney. Stop yelling at yourself to "just get up" when you are dying. Your oxygen mask of forgiveness is now on. When you judge yourself for suffering, you are pinching the oxygen cord and restricting the flow of life to your dying body. When you think judgmental thoughts about yourself or your body you are grinding your heel into your pain. It's kicking yourself when you are down. You can stop now. It's time to run free. Dissolution of judgment in this moment is a gift that is accepted with compassion.

When a thought to eat emerged, I checked my hunger scale in my stomach. If I was above a four, I began to become aware of other needs, needs I usually fed with food. Before my pregnancy, I rarely let myself feel stomach hunger. I usually ate to treat an emotional or physical need. I began to satisfy each need with the proper treatment. I would ask myself how I felt. Was I tired, lonely, bored or anxious? Oftentimes before pregnancy, when I had an uncomfortable thought or feeling, I would judge it as being wrong or invalid, which would lead to fear or denial. Resistance compounded the feelings. I heard Marianne Williamson once say, "What you resist persists". Being pregnant was the first time I consistently allowed myself to have a range of "negative" feelings or thoughts without judging them by saying "you shouldn't feel...or think....." I knew that I was supposed to be emotional, tired and physically sick a lot, so when these feelings came up I embraced them with the love and compassion of being pregnant. I knew I was supposed to be feeling "negative" emotions. Nothing was "wrong" with me for feeling emotional, sick or tired. There was no reason to feel afraid of these emotions or thoughts. I was exactly the way I was supposed to be. My "just being human" before my pregnancy was never a valid enough reason to feel the feelings without judgment.

I also knew now that the discomfort would pass. Before, I had an unrealistic fear that the uncomfortable feelings had moved into my body with a 30 year mortgage. Crazy. It became natural to rest when I was tired. I was respecting my body's signals. Before when I was tired, I would eat to wake myself up, which worked for five minutes until I felt heavier and slower than before I ate. I realized that having needs or feeling a certain way is a normal, healthy part of being human. Judging a thought, feeling, or circumstance, in the moment, as unacceptable created the intolerable discomfort that demanded to be fed.

Thoughts of acceptance and love dissolve the need to eat over being human. I learned to open the door and embrace the feelings in front of me without judgment and be free, instead of resisting what's in the present moment, then feeling worse and overeating. Instead of being afraid of my thoughts and feelings, or saying I shouldn't be feeling or thinking a certain way, I welcomed and hugged the feelings. I actually visualized little feelings knocking on my door! I imagined opening the door, letting them scurry in, then picking them up and embracing them with compassion.

I knew on a deeper level that the feelings were harmless and they were just passing through. Having consistent IHA moments is when I began to experience the peace Eckhart Tolle writes about in *The Power of*

Now. I started becoming friends with the present moment by talking to it. With judgment no longer blocking the way for love and healing to flow through, the affirmations and self - talk I learned years earlier began to change my relationship with myself and my world. I looked in the mirror and said, "I love you Amy, I really love you," and actually felt love instead of judgment. In becoming friends with the present moment, I would thank each part of my body for working so well and began to feel gratitude and sincere appreciation flow through my body. To say, "Hi present moment, come on in, let's play together," was a great way to surrender with love to what is.

When I want to eat when I'm not hungry, I ask myself if I'm judging something in the moment as unacceptable. For example, in looking at the reality of the moment of feeling sick, I learned that I could actually be at peace with feeling sick, knowing it would pass. I could look around at what I actually liked about the moment. " What do I have more of than I even need right now?" counters the wanting of more. Saying out loud, "I like what I have right now" (mobility, sight, a car) opens the door for the light of the moment to sparkle on and warm my body. My chest feels tight and my breathing is shallow when I'm resisting the moment so I began to stand up straight, put my hands to my chest and pretend I'm opening the double doors of my chest to let the light of possibility pour into my body.

When my mind is in a state of dis-ease, restlessness and judgment and I feed it with food, then I never feel satisfied and always need more.

When my mind is at peace with the moment and I've met my other needs, the desire to eat occurs only when my stomach signals hunger.

During my pregnancy, I began to experience a dramatic shift in consciousness from the cluttered chatter in my mind to the sense of awe and wonder in my body. The force in my body is working 24/7 to keep me moving and healthy. It never needs a break and asks me to take over. What a gift this energy is in my body and it took me years to acknowledge and really appreciate it. Have you ever thought of the generosity of the force, or the God within? Think of all it's doing for you even when we mistreat it!

When I began my transfer of awareness from my fears and judgments in my head to the miracle in my body, my mind became more peaceful. I began practicing body consciousness by paying attention to any sensations in my belly. I began to affirm, "My natural state is magic and brilliance inside. My body works perfectly." My mind created thoughts that buried the ball of bliss inside me with food because I just didn't know yet that I had fireworks, sunsets, music, -God- inside my body. I put my attention on each part of my body from my feet to my head and identified any tingling sensation or movement inside. How does my body feel inside? What are the colors inside? Do I feel any energy moving in my fingers? I began to have images of what was happening inside my body. For years, I saw my body as an empty vessel, or just a dark, sludgy, heavy blob. I now started to see a party in my body! Seriously! All the little cells running through my blood vessels on their way to my heart, all working together just as happy as can be. I saw fireworks shooting up from my feet and showering into my head and down my chest over my whole body and how delighted all the little cells were to feel it. When I'm outside, I imagine the sun sparkling magic onto my body and feel the warmth and know its God. With each inhale I imagine my lungs filling up with sparkly light and when I exhale I blow that sparkly light out into my room or onto my children and I imagine what it looks like.

The feelings of ease, comfort and security that I craved to connect to with food, I realized were already alive inside me. I just had to learn how to pause, connect to and activate the release of those feelings from the inside. I didn't have to "eat it"; it already lives inside my body! What I've looked for in food, alcohol, drugs, relationships etc. was inside all along, I just forgot! The truth is, after I binged on food to feel ease and comfort, the post binge blues always followed. I always felt numb, less alive, heavy, more alone and afraid. I began to access the good feelings already alive inside by remembering times when I felt peace, joy or exhilaration without ingesting an outside substance. Running and listening to music has oftentimes activated and released the feeling of bliss from my core. The feelings have been so overwhelming that I get goose bumps and I cry. The feeling of gratitude and euphoria has been so powerful that it took my breath away. I have felt peace just as powerful after a hectic day, when the house is clean and quiet, and I'm finally in my warm, cozy bed reading a book I love, knowing that I can completely relax. I also experienced a party in my body, the alive, vibrating, pulsing, light energy filling me so completely that there was no room for food. And I realized that the last thing I wanted was to put too much food in my body and risk burying the party!

Another thing I discovered living in my body is a sedative. For fifteen years a leaf blower lived in my head. At any moment it turned on, blew thoughts all over, making a mess and polluting my head. Or my head sometimes felt like a pinball machine. It would be still for a minute but as soon as an obsessive thought was shot out, it touched all kinds of bells and whistles, sending it to worse places. Now when my thoughts are busy, I can actually imagine a sedative released in my head, filling it with a still peaceful ocean at sunset and the feeling of relaxation is activated.

So when I think back at how at odds I was with my body I see that my mind hated my body. My mind was simply unaware of God's energy inside my body. I saw only the tiniest fraction of what was happening in my body. The extra weight was just a result of my not knowing the truth that everything (all the energy) I ever wanted (God) was alive and well inside me. So now the last thing I want to do is put extra food in my body that would dull the magic. My state of mind began to shift from one of judgment to one of loving acceptance.

When you lose judgment, you lose weight. Judging your body, thoughts and feelings in the present moment creates dis – ease, which you've attempted to comfort with food. By becoming conscious in the moment, you have the opportunity to dissolve judgment into compassion. Judgment makes whatever "is" not good enough or wrong. You are saying that what "is" is not acceptable and you won't be ok until it changes. The truth is: change happens in a quicker, more powerful way when it comes from compassion. Judgment simply blocks power. It's an obstruction in the flow. So open the door, let the feelings in, pick them up and hug them. Embracing discomfort with compassion dissolves judgment into love.

The HOW:

1. **Identify** what you are feeling in the moment, for example: anxious, tired, hopeful, lonely, sad, peaceful

2. **Honor** the feelings: hold your feelings, no matter what they are, with the utmost respect, and appreciate what they are trying to tell you.

3. **Allow** the feelings: to be as long as they need to be, knowing that they will pass when they've served their purpose. They can be telling you how to take better care of your body (rest if you are tired, exercise if you feel like your energy level is low).Emotions often give us clues to what we are thinking and what the beliefs are at the root of the thoughts, which will be discussed in chapters eight and nine.

Chapter 7

Plant the Seeds of Possibility

"Create the highest, grandest vision possible for your life because you become what you believe."

- Oprah Winfrey

A simple belief in possibility is enough to crack open the door to freedom. The moment you are willing to pause and declare, "I believe it's possible to feel comfort without using food" is the moment power begins to flow. Possibility opens the door for feelings of hope to wash away despair. Be willing to believe that if I am free from compulsive overeating, then it is possible for you too. That maybe one day you will naturally eat only when your stomach is hungry and stop when satisfied. Let that light of possibility shine on you for a minute. Just consider waiting to eat until your stomach is hungry. Your stomach might need several hours to clear

177

out before it needs food again. Consider letting your body's brilliance take over. Consider believing it's possible to feel so full of power, enthusiasm for life, love for people, and peace inside that the thought of eating outside of stomach hunger is ridiculous and the idea of overeating is repulsive. I ate for the possibility of feeling better until I realized that possibility already lives inside me just waiting to be activated. Did you stuff food inside your belly hoping to feel ease and comfort? Do you believe it's possible to feel the feelings you crave without using food? You can plug into food for a connection and deprive yourself, or you can plug into and connect with possibility inside and feel hope rising in your heart. You are pregnant with possibility!

I've heard people say "Anything is possible." They might be right, but I think two kinds of possibilities exist: "pipe dream" possibilities and practical possibilities. "Pipe dream" possibilities for me would include becoming an airplane pilot or competing in an Ironman race. Sure those goals are possible, but unlikely for me. What I'm talking about here is practical possibility. If you've been compulsively eating for years, *becoming free is a practical possibility for you.* Experiencing bliss inside depends on your belief in possibility. Consider the following practical possibilities for your life:

It's possible for me to rarely think about food.

It's possible for me to lose weight easily.

It's possible for me to eat when I'm hungry and stop before I'm too full.

It's possible for me to LOVE my body.

It's possible to feel my feelings and let them pass without eating.

It's possible to feel comfort without food.

It's possible to experience peace of mind most of the time.

It's possible for me to feel comfortable in my skin.

It's possible that I can exercise today even though I don't feel like it.

It's possible that there are ways to create and make more money beyond what I can see right now.

It's possible to feel rested and restored without "enough" sleep.

It's possible that I can feel peaceful and relaxed throughout the day until my head hits the pillow.

It's possible that I can show more love to people today than yesterday.

It's possible for me to experience freedom from food and from my body.

It's possible to activate my Bellyful of Bliss.

When we remember an experience that made us feel angry or upset, we can actually start feeling angry or upset all over again. I bought a car a few years ago and the moment I drove it off the lot, one of the bumper lights fell out, dangling as I drove down the street. Over the next month, I took it to get repaired four times. Each time, the service department promised it was fixed and each time I was surprised and angry when it fell out again. After driving away from the dealership for the fourth time realizing it was still broken, I drove back to the dealer, told them once again that they had not fixed it properly and asked if I was being punk'd or caught on candid camera. It was that absurd. The dealer also said they fixed the stereo and a few weeks later the same problem occurred. Lastly, they sold me the wrong warranty. When I am reminded of this experience I feel my chest tighten and I start to feel angry again. It's easy to re-feel anger from the past. In the same way we re-feel negative emotions, we can just as easily wake up positive emotions and give them life again. When you feel positive feelings like awe and wonder in the moment, the desire to eat is dissolved. It is possible for you to re-feel God in the moment of wanting to eat. I realized that when I feel trapped and isolated at night in my apartment, I can imagine my favorite run and feel the stored feelings of freedom, as I sit in my living room. When I'm bored, I can stop and remember David Bowie singing to me under the stars at The Greek Theater and feel the exhilaration that brought me to tears years earlier.

When I've had a hectic day and reach my limit of stress I can stop, become aware of peace in my belly by visualizing my favorite relaxing experience which is getting a massage, then release that feeling, or energy into my whole body. It's like watching fireworks – you light the wick, it shoots up into the sky, then light showers down with beautiful grace. With practice, it is possible to allow space in your stomach, hear what it really needs and activate the power to feel the feelings you crave.

You can also imagine a future feeling and release it into your body to activate power. One feeling I imagine is buying a two story house with a yard in a neighborhood that I love. I see myself cozy in my fluffy bed, looking out my bedroom window at the treetops. That activates feelings of excitement, hope and comfort. Those feelings empower me to keep writing and working on other projects to make money. For years I felt hope from other people's stories of success. I now have my own experiences to release those feelings inside when I'm willing to pause and remember the power of possibility. Now your bliss begins to bubble, your spark starts to sparkle, and your light begins to shine! Plant your seeds of possibility now.

The HOW:

1. Write your list of possibilities.

2. Write about an experience when you felt full of yummy feelings. Was it when you were a child and you were excited about school starting, or summer camp? You knew possibility existed. Or when you got your first job and you could see yourself saving your money to buy something you always wanted. What are your most positively charged memories?

3. Write about an experience in the future that you are looking forward to. What are your goals, hopes and wishes?

Chapter 8

Identify Beliefs that are Burying Your Bliss

"Until you make the unconscious conscious, it will direct your life..."

- Carl Jung

"Why did I just binge?" is the question that baffled me for years. The only answer I had was that eating made me feel better in the moment. It gave me a sense of ease and comfort, but why was I in a state of dis-ease when nothing "bad" had even happened before the binge?

Your beliefs form your state of consciousness. Thoughts arise out of your state of consciousness, which create your feelings. I believed for a few years that I was powerless over food because I couldn't control my eating. At one point, I was told that I was powerless over my thoughts and feelings and I believed it. These beliefs spiraled me down deep into despair. I was in a delusion that I lacked God's power. I also suffered from a limiting belief that God was somewhere outside me, that I was separate from God. These beliefs created tremendous fear and pain. Seeds of belief can grow at remarkable speed. When fear grows roots in the fertile ground of your head, it spreads like weeds where snakes slither around.

As I described in chapter three, one of my longstanding negative beliefs was that being tired sapped my power source and dulled my thinking. I believed that feeling tired meant nothing good would really come from the day. My best shot was just to somehow make it through until I could sleep again, then I might have a chance for a good day tomorrow. What I perceived that I lacked was power and opportunity for productivity. Food was my power substitute. I would actually feel a slight surge of energy when I thought about eating chocolate. I would feel hope that I was about to feel a connection from outside of myself to a perceived lack of power inside. The idea that hope, relief or comfort lived inside of me simply did not exist. I believed that feeling tired meant that I lacked access to creative energy, mental alertness and physical strength. I ate to get the fleeting rush, then I would feel heavier and slower as my world shrunk. Until I questioned the validity of this belief, I treated feeling tired with food. Walt Whitman has been quoted as saying, "Reexamine everything you've been told. Dismiss whatever insults your soul."

The day you question whether a self defeating belief is really true is the day you begin to experience freedom and power. Most beliefs are unconsciously downloaded in childhood from other people, without your permission.

I'd known people who could sleep fewer hours than me and still have a productive day working, exercising and having fun with friends. I began to wonder if it was possible for me to be like those people. Being tired didn't determine the quality of their day. How was that? They clearly held a different belief. They simply lived a full day whether they got a full eight or not. For years I believed that my body was different from theirs, that I had a different "makeup". I was forced to question the validity of my belief after my son was born. Being awake every few hours and up early in the morning was a recipe for being tired and using food to get through the day for at least the first year of his life. I knew that wouldn't work for me. I knew I had to adjust to feeling good without enough sleep. I decided to change my belief.

I began to unravel the knots in my head of negative beliefs, as I listed in chapter three. All of my limited, helpless, at the mercy of an unstable authority figure are old. These beliefs originated from being sixteen, stuck in my room, raging at Dad and Mom. I felt angry and insecure. I felt like I was stuck and alone in an expressionless place. I felt powerless in my life. I also felt like my opinions and feelings didn't matter. I saw clearly that those beliefs from years ago were unconsciously affecting my eating and financial security in my twenties. I was not that sixteen year old girl anymore, I did not consciously choose the negative beliefs, and I decided that once I identified them, I could delete the beliefs that created negative thoughts, feelings and actions. I knew other people who had done this exercise and it worked for them, so why not me?

The HOW:

1. Remember when you first began compulsively eating. What was happening in your life at that time? Now identify what your beliefs were about what was happening. You will see that many of these beliefs are at the root of your pain that is creating the need to compulsively eat today.

2. The next time you want to eat outside of stomach hunger, practice disciplines one-four, then ask yourself, what are the thoughts behind the feelings? What am I thinking right now? Where did that thought come from? What is the belief at the root of that thought? Did I choose that belief with a mature, sane mind? Is that belief even true today?

3. Make a list of your beliefs about food, your body, God, your potential, your relationships, work, etc. Identifying your negative beliefs gives you the choice to delete them and replace them with positive beliefs.

Chapter 9

Create the Life You Crave, One Belief at a Time

"Our belief at the beginning of a doubtful undertaking is the one thing that insures the successful outcome of your venture."

-William James

In a moment of wanting to eat, you can open your mouth or open your mind, and it's your choice.

What you are craving is much yummier than food. If your soul was truly aching for food, you would feel happy and content after a binge, instead of feeling weak and depressed. Without filling your body with unneeded food, your intuitive voice becomes louder and clearer. What at first is just the faint sound of stomach hunger, you will now begin to hear as creative intelligence inside. See each desire to eat outside of stomach hunger as an announcement from your Spirit. Your Spirit is trying to tell you that there's a positive belief that fits better than the old belief. It's often the failure to identify what you truly want that hurts. When you ignore your Spirit, you feel discomfort. Not listening to the divinity within hurts. Settling for a mediocre life is painful. Looking at a negative belief with curiosity gives you the opportunity to identify, perhaps for the first time, what it is you really want. When I listened, my spirit announced that my soul had a need to express its purpose in a powerful, creative, passionate way that would be absolutely exhilarating and fulfilling beyond what I ever hoped or dreamed from a pint of ice cream. That is my truth today!

A world of creativity lives inside each desire to compulsively eat. It's in that moment that a new belief has the opportunity to be manifested. I love affirmations and they helped me to have a positive attitude on many occasions. As Ralph Waldo Emerson stated, "A man is what he thinks about all day long". What I discovered though, is that I can use positive affirmations all day long, but that's like using a lawn mower to cut weeds. If I don't pull the negative thoughts (weeds) out from the roots (my beliefs), they continue to emerge. I saturated my mind with new beliefs and the faith that change was already happening inside. Replacing each negative belief with a positive belief will satiate your hunger with a personal purpose and inner power beyond your expectations. You will see that all the s**t beliefs that caused the pain of your eating disorder now provide the rich field of fertilizer for the seeds of the new, healthier beliefs to grow. From what seemed like a big pile of manure now grows a beautiful, vibrant garden full of life and creativity.

The HOW:

You have been depriving yourself with each compulsive bite. Just as your body needs healthy food to thrive, your brain needs positive beliefs to live your best life. Fill your head, or fill your stomach:

1. Use your imagination to describe how you want to be. How do you want to live now? If that sounds far out just remember, you've been using your imagination for years in a negative way to create negative thoughts, feelings and experiences.

2. Now it's time to take each negative belief on your list and turn it into your list of positive beliefs.

Chapter 10

My Freedom Today

"The wondrous change that comes over us as we gradually realize what the Omnipresence of God really means, transfigures every phase of our lives, turning sorrow into joy, age into youth, and dullness into light and life. This is the glory – and the glory which comes to us is, of course, God's too. And the bliss we know in that experience is still God Himself, who is knowing that bliss through us."

- Emmett Fox

I have not gotten stuck in the obsessive binge- deprivation- depression cycle in over seven years. Can you believe that?! I used to think "I just need a new brain and a new body." I thought that because I was so deeply stuck that if I was lucky, the best case scenario for my life would be to learn how to cope with my eating disorder with a more positive attitude, come to terms with a body I was not proud of, and maybe experience a few moments here and there of peace of mind. Well, I do have a new brain and a new body today. The freedom I have experienced on a daily basis for the past seven years far surpasses any way of life I hoped for during my fifteen years of suffering.

In honoring stomach hunger and fullness, I can eat whatever I want without gaining weight, without creating a mental obsession for more and without guilt. Just as I allow myself to eat whatever I like, I am also allowing myself to believe I can experience whatever I like in my life. That tastes even better! When I don't eat when I'm not hungry, I'm saying that I want something better than food and I'm going to get exactly what I want for myself. I'm not settling for food when I want something that's truly satisfying.

I love that my mornings are peaceful now. I don't wake up hungover or depressed from a binge the night before. One morning I woke up and the sun was bursting through the window and I felt like I was part of the light and all the sparkles and light lived in my body. They are now shining through me! I am so humbled.

Living from a Bellyful of Bliss is like floating on a raft. You know I struggled for a long time. During the struggle I had spiritual experiences that were like stepping stones from the desert to the ocean. I just float and enjoy the sunshine most of the time. Now, when a wave knocks me off my raft, I tread water or swim through the discomfort until I'm back on my raft.

I see that the fifteen years of torturous fear drove me into my spiritual experiences. The power behind my fear is what propelled me right smack into my freedom! I thank God today for my fear and pain. If I had just been meandering in a state of semi-comfort, I don't think I would have searched so desperately for God. My appetite for food was insatiable because I was really craving personal power from spiritual satiation. I feel that I was graced with pain because it turned into the gift of freedom.

Freedom from compulsive eating was just the beginning for me. I thought being free from overeating and obsessing about food and my body was the end all, be all. That was the dream goal of my life: to not think about food and be naturally thin. What I discovered beyond the "freedom from" is a world of "freedom to" just waiting for me. The "freedom to" is endless because it lies in God's infinite sea of possibility. Matthew 19:26 states, "With God all things are possible." Wayne Dyer loves to ask, "What does that leave out?"

*****

My runs became deeper spiritual experiences. I was listening to Slash's solo album, "Slash", thinking about the physical reaction I had the first time I heard it. I felt shivers all over my body and cried a few tears of awe. When I listened again on my run, it took my breath away for a second, and then I felt chills on the top of my head. It lasted for about twenty seconds, which felt like a long time, but not long enough! The crown of my head was tingling! I thought to myself, "I didn't just feel chills on top of my head! How is that even possible? " I've felt goose bumps everywhere on my body but never on the top of my head! It was such a trippy experience. The coolest part was that I had become friends with Slash and his wife Perla a few years earlier, so I was able to call him and share my experience and gratitude personally. He so graciously accepted the compliment. You might not know it, but he has one of the sweetest hearts in Hollywood.

I love to watch the music channel, Palladia, on TV. They play awesome live concerts daily, mostly rock and roll. It reminds me of MTV when it first aired in the eighties. Anyway, I was watching Metallica play with many special guests when Ozzy took the stage to play "Iron Man". My son Bowie, who was five at the time, said of James Hetfield, "Mommy look, that guy is playing guitar and chewing gum at the same time!" I said, "Well that guy singing with the black eyeliner gave me a piece of gum one time!" He was surprised and impressed when I told him the story:

When I walked into the Key Club on Sunset to meet some friends, only a few seats were available. One was next to Ozzy, so of course I took it! I had taken an orange with me in case I got hungry. I was trying so hard to wait for the hunger, but back then hungry still represented an out of control, vulnerable emptiness. I peeled my orange and offered Ozzy a slice. He politely declined and offered me a piece of gum, which I gratefully accepted! Being in the presence of insanely talented legends, like Ozzy, blew up energy inside that I could not control. Eating that orange was enough to satisfy my hunger but it wasn't nearly enough to ground the storm brewing inside. I had so much creativity swirling around inside me and I didn't yet know how to channel it. I didn't even know it was creative energy at the time. The only way I could ground myself was to weigh myself down with food.

Sometimes it was like a fire that I only knew how to control by smothering it with food. I didn't know then that the fire blazing within was my spirit. It scared me because it was powerful and too bright for my eyes to see. I'm not afraid of the storm or the fire today. I have the power to choose to plug into and connect with my bellyful of bliss to ground me. From there I can peacefully create a channel for creativity to flow out in a positive way. You have a choice to plug into food, or the peace inside your belly.

My spirit sometimes felt like a wild stallion running rampant inside of me. It felt like it was too big for my body and wore me out. Over time, I lost the fear that horses can so easily sense and I gained respect and curiosity. I learned how to ride that stallion in the direction of my dreams. Once you learn how to ride, watch out, you're going to go somewhere fast!

*****

Lady Gaga penetrated my being and spoke straight to my spirit as I ran east up San Vicente. I was listening to "Born This Way" and "You and I". My breathing was deep and heavy, I could feel my blood pumping and I was aware of my bellyful of bliss. I was connected to it and fully charged. As I approached 17th street, it struck me that God was in my blood. I could feel God pumping through every vein in my body: through my arms, legs, head, feet- everywhere! I felt God rushing through my blood. It was the most exhilarating feeling and one I never imagined. The next knowing I had was that God had moved from my gut into my heart. God was in the center of my heart, pumping through my entire body! God was the life in my body! It took my breath away and I stopped on the sidewalk and cried. The tears were about being graced with a new experience that was absolutely euphoric. The arresting beauty of God's presence is literally breathtaking. What is so profound is the dramatically different experience I'm having in my body and my mind. For years I was trying to outrun my demons and now I'm running with an awareness of God inside that feels like the grand finale of fireworks on the 4th of July. I am in awe of God's power. To be free from compulsive eating with a relatively still, quiet head is astonishing. I am proof that anything is possible.

*****

Of course, not every day is goose bumps and fireworks. The discomfort I feel today doesn't drive me into a binge, but every once in a while it does create a desire to eat outside of stomach hunger. Discomfort is simply an announcement from my spirit. Sometimes it's telling me a belief is not in alignment with love, and sometimes I just chalk it up to a reminder that I'm a spiritual being having a human experience.

A friend who is struggling with compulsive eating was telling me that she has determined many of her triggers for discomfort. She was grateful that now she can avoid those situations that make her want to eat. She called herself a "comfort junkie" with no tolerance for discomfort. She also mentioned that she didn't feel safe in the world and felt anxious a lot.

I told her that I could definitely identify because I spent years trying to avoid uncomfortable feelings and comfort myself with food. I explained that I felt like I was at the mercy of the discomfort. Sometimes it would creep up on me like an itch I couldn't scratch and other times it would jump out as a surprise attack. It reminded me of trying to keep balls underwater. Knowing that discomfort is part of the human experience and unavoidable at times is actually comforting to me now.

I told my friend that when I began to discover the power inside me, the monster of discomfort started to shrink. Eckhart Tolle talks about being the observer of your thoughts and feelings. Paramahansa Yogananda, the founder of the Self Realization Fellowship, and author of "Autobiography of a Yogi" writes about the idea that we are not our bodies or our thoughts. As I've become more aware of the God energy inside me, I've become more detached from my discomfort. I am more tuned into the peace and power inside than the discomfort. I am not afraid of discomfort anymore, nor do I go out of my way to avoid it. I don't welcome it but it doesn't have power over me. I told my friend that when I slow down long enough to listen, I realized that I had negative beliefs, which created scary thoughts, which created discomfort. Since I've changed my beliefs, I'm comfortable in my skin most of the time. I'm astounded that I can say that but it's absolutely true. I lived for years feeling like crawling out of my skin, now it fits perfectly!

The monster of discomfort has shrunk down to a benign little mouse. The mouse scurries around outside of me. It doesn't live in my head or my body. I can watch it run around and hide and even feel compassion for it. If that can happen for me, it can happen for you.

*****

The other day the chatter in my mind sounded like, "I don't know what to do today. I want to eat chocolate but I'm not hungry. Maybe I should drive to Malibu and take a walk." That door closes. No. "Maybe I should go look for a bathing suit. No. It will be too crowded." That door closes. "I want to be somewhere else NOW! Feeling peace NOW!" What I saw was an image of my thoughts as little ego gremlins, jumping up from the ground onto my feet. Crawling up my calves saying all these things – driving me crazy! Then I realized that my thoughts are not me, they're just little pesky gremlins – and when I see them like that, the light in my body radiates and they fall off dissolving in the light. The thoughts are not inside me. They're not in me or a part of me. They are superficial. They're crawling on my skin, trying to snuggle. They can never get inside, or under my skin, but they can attach themselves to me if I let them. I can choose to detach from my thoughts and return to the peace that lives in my mind.

Later in a workshop, I was talking about putting a pause between the desire to eat and the first bite, to practice the six disciplines. One of the attendees raised her hand and said it was just so much easier to eat at the end of a long stressful day with her kids, than to make the effort to pause. She said that eating was fast, guaranteed comfort. So I asked myself the same question. Why not eat? It is quick comfort. The answer was clear. My level of pain associated with bingeing finally determined my level of willingness to pause. The gift in that is that my level of willingness is directly proportional to my level of freedom. The depth and expanse of my freedom is a result of my spiritual seeking. My degree of pain was a gift because I'm now living in a state of freedom that I never imagined, and it actually exceeds the depth of the pain! I heard things along the way that confirm my experience such as, "Pain is the touchstone of spiritual progress." Ok, so what's so great about spiritual growth? It's freedom, an inner freedom that no one can take from you. It's a sense of awe and wonder. It's a feeling of being comfortable in your skin – most of the time. It's the ability to feel peace and gratitude inside disappointment. It's thinking less about yourself and more about others. It's feeling joy bubble up from deep within. It's feeling so much love for someone else that it brings tears to your eyes. It's feeling so much peace inside stillness that you don't even want to move. It's a profound appreciation for life – your own and every living thing. It's not being afraid of pain. It's feeling so full of gratitude that you want for nothing. It's becoming aware of the bliss inside and learning how to release it into the world on a daily basis. It's the most valuable gift that you can't buy. It's everything I've ever wanted, and more. That's what spiritual growth means to me, and I've just begun.

*****

A few months ago, as I felt space in my stomach, I saw my hunger as a sexy, slinking, Sofia Vergara slowly emerging from the foggy darkness. I laughed to myself and decided to wait a few more minutes until she got closer. I wanted to see her up close and hear her growl! Needless to say, I am no longer afraid to feel hungry. I welcome it and I love to satisfy my hunger with food I love.

My family and I love to eat at Swingers on Sundays. My son and I usually order the vegan multi - grain chocolate chip pancakes. One morning I noticed that my stomach was satisfied after eating two of the three pancakes but I wanted to keep eating more. I looked at that last pancake and I felt like I was leaving a piece of my heart on the plate. As if I could only have a small portion of the yummiest most feel good stuff. It was a bit heartbreaking. I stayed connected and discovered that what I really wanted was a large order of delicious nurturing. I knew I wouldn't get that from the third pancake. It's not about what I want to put in my stomach; it's about what's already alive inside. I went deeper. I looked around inside myself and discovered that I wanted to feel hope and inspiration for a career that I'm passionate about. I affirmed my belief that I AM creating it with my thoughts and actions. What else did I really want in my life? A deeper connection to love in other people. I want to belly laugh unexpectedly. I want to feel the comfort of my comfy pajamas after a warm bath. I want the feeling of relaxation from a massage. The feeling of physical strength when I run and the feeling of pride and accomplishment when I'm finished. When I listened to my Spirit tell me what it wanted, the third pancake paled in comparison. I left Swingers satisfied AND fulfilled.

Discomfort is a reminder today that I have the power of choice. I have the power to choose to feel uncomfortable without eating to quell my anxiety. It is powerful to choose to feel the discomfort and untangle it. It's my tour guide for this human experience of life. If I listen, it gives me precise direction on how to get through obstacles. Seeing life as an adventure with obstacle courses can be fun if you remember that you are not running a race, you are playing on a playground.

*****

On June 4th, 2010 at 6:30am, I woke up before my three year old son well rested, excited about my first morning in Hawaii. As I sat in meditation I asked, as I had for months, what the name of this book should be. I remember Eckhart Tolle talking to Oprah about the creative process on the online telecast based on his book *A New Earth*. He explained that when he sat down to write *The Power of Now*, he knew the book was already written, it just needed his hand to flow through onto the page. In that energy of asking, relaxing and allowing, I closed my eyes and within 30 seconds *A Bellyful of Bliss* filled my awareness. I knew that was the right name for my book just as I knew my own name. I felt a sparkly, invigorating peace wash over me and I was once again surprised at the clarity with which I was receiving a message from the Creative Intelligence. It was as if another light turned on in my body. Slowly but surely I was lighting up, with each spiritual experience.

A few hours later as I played with my son in the water of Waikiki Beach, my husband called my name and as I turned and waved, he took the bikini picture you can view on my website. That was a spontaneous, candid moment that required no preparation.

I never felt comfortable in a bikini during my years of compulsive eating because my "fat head" was so loud. I was afraid you could see my fear and vulnerability. I felt like you could see what I was doing to myself in secret and the shame was suffocating. The anxiety of preparing to be "bikini ready" was always relieved by a binge when the bikini came off.

The photo at Waikiki Beach represents freedom. Instead of a life of spontaneous bingeing, I now live a life of spontaneous fun. I'm just as bikini ready December 26th as I am July 4th. There's no preparation and no anxiety. I have cellulite and a few stretch marks. I'm proud of my "imperfect" body! It's carried and nursed two babies. I felt just as comfortable July 4th, 2011 six weeks post-partum, with extra weight in my bikini, as I felt July 4th 2012 with no extra weight. I feel free in a bathing suit and so can you. I am in awe of my state of mental and emotional freedom, and I'm humbled by the physical manifestation of my spiritual growth.

*****

When I read Eckhart Tolle's *A New Earth*, I had my own experience with what he calls "the animating presence blazing within." I closed my eyes, looked inside and saw a pink cloud of consciousness. A p-c-o-c! It was a pulsing vibrating, pink cloud with white light shining through. I knew it was God inside me and I could feel the warmth and see the light radiating out from my core. I opened my eyes and looked at people around me and laughed as I said to myself "I see your p-c-o-c!" I felt a Universal connection with people in a way that I had never felt before.

It's up to you how fast you get free. The more you saturate your body with forgiveness, the faster your blocks of self loathing will dissolve. Every time you release judgment and have an IHA moment, you will need to eat less. Every time you listen for stomach hunger, your intuition will mute the obsessive chatter in your head. Believe in possibility. Why not? Replace negative beliefs with positive beliefs. It's a win- win situation! You can practice the disciplines every day as a mantra, or only when you feel discomfort. Either way, you'll get free. How long have you been in prison? How willing are you to make the effort? How ready are you to feel pride in your body? Do you want to live before you die? Uncover and discover your Bellyful of Bliss; it's just the beginning of a life better than you could plan.

Chapter 11

Tools to Activate Your Inner Yummy

1. Recapturing your child-like spirit: Remember before you began compulsively eating. Describe your thoughts and feelings about food and your body.

Begin to remember your playful, carefree moments as a child. Describe your childlike spirit.

What did you like to do for fun?

What was your favorite game/activity/sport?

What made you laugh as a child?

Describe your "happy place" as a child. It could also be a place where you felt the most comfortable.

If you can't remember everything, one memory is enough to reconnect with your childlike spirit.

2. Identify one yummy thing to look forward to each day, instead of food.

3. Obsess on gratitude.

4. Visualize your day, believing that you can feel full and at peace with every activity. Visualize going to sleep with a clean, clear body, at a "6" on the hunger scale. Visualize yourself waking up full of energy and hope.

5. Express your creativity.

6. Move your body to release endorphins.

7. Meditate to feel the peace and perfection of a sleeping baby. You are connected to the unshakable stillness inside.

Afterword

The less I feel like I need, the more I appreciate what I have. It's interesting. When I don't need more from people or more from the material world, I feel a sense of awe and wonder because of the fact that I'm healthy, my family is healthy and we live in a safe, comfortable apartment in a city that I love. I am aware that I'm not entitled to any of these things. Because I have the use of all five senses, I can walk, and talk, and I live in a free country, I feel like I've hit the jackpot. If nothing "good" ever happens for me again in my life, I have enough good today to last me a lifetime. That's why I can say that I'm grateful for the fifteen years of suffering with compulsive eating. During that time I told God that if I could just live free from the mental obsession with food and my body and the bingeing that followed, that I wouldn't need anything else. Freedom would be enough for me to live a happy life. I've received so many gifts as a result of the pain of compulsive eating, but one of the biggest gifts is the gift of perspective. I am free today. The rest is gravy.

When I look back, I see that the freedom I experience today began during my last years of bingeing. It's clear to me now that all the work I did with the disciplines preceded my present freedom from compulsive eating. The naturally thin and healthy body I love today is a result of the years of inner work. I love that I am more conscious of my peace of mind than my body. The love I feel inside is more valuable to me than what I see on the outside. It IS an inside job. The worst thing you can do is beat yourself up after a binge. If you want to take the fast track to freedom, celebrate the "small changes" just as you would celebrate a baby's first steps. It's time to be your own cheerleader. Jump up and down, do cartwheels each time you wait for hunger and stop eating before you are too full. You know the baby is going to walk each time she gets up after a fall, and I know you can become free.

Acknowledgements

First, I'd like to thank Gary Adams for supporting me during the three years I spent writing this book. Thank you for believing in me and taking care of our kids on your days off work so I could write. You are the best and I'm forever grateful to you. Thanks to my son, Bowie and my daughter, Layla for being my angels of motivation.

Thanks to my parents for their love and support. Thanks especially to my Mom for always listening when I needed to talk and for inspiring me with pep talks when I was discouraged. Mom, you are my rock, my example of unconditional love, and I am eternally grateful to you.

Thanks to Carey Williams, Jamie Rose, Michael Lally, Judith Orloff, and everyone at my writer's group in the Palisades. Thanks to Hillary Cramer for the back cover Author Photo. Finally, thanks to all the spiritual teachers whose books guided me on my road to freedom.

Thank you God.

Printed in Great Britain
by Amazon.co.uk, Ltd.,
Marston Gate.